THE ROSARY AND DEVOTION TO MARY

The *Rosary* and *Devotion* to *Mary*

by Deacon Andrew J. Gerakas

St. Paul Books & Media

Nihil Obstat:
    Rev. Marc Alexander

Imprimatur:
    + Joseph A. Ferrario
    Bishop of Honolulu

Library of Congress Cataloging-in-Publication Data

Gerakas, Andrew J.
    The Rosary and devotion to Mary / by Andrew J. Gerakas.
    ISBN 0-8198-6417-X
    1. Rosary.   I. Title.
    BX2163.G43 1988   88-11319
    242'.74—dc19   CIP

Printed and published in the U.S.A. by St. Paul Books & Media
50 St. Paul's Avenue, Boston, MA 02130

St. Paul Books & Media is the publishing house of the Daughters of St. Paul, an international
congregation of women religious serving the Church with the communications media.

2 3 4 5 6 7 8 9   99 98 97 96 95 94 93 92

Contents

Foreword

The Rosary is a sublime prayer, blessed by God from ancient times and praised by saints, scholars, popes, priests and lay persons as a rich means of obtaining God's grace and mercy.

This little book by Andrew J. Gerakas, Deacon of the Diocese of Honolulu, reviews the history of the Rosary, cites many endorsements of it as an eminently beneficial form of prayer, and explains why and how it is so special in the history of Christianity. How to say the Rosary, in varied ways, is also treated.

Throughout the volume the unique status of Mary as Mother of God and Mother of the Church—through whom all blessings flow from Christ her Son—is clarified. The author explains the richness of the Rosary devotion throughout the ages, and discusses the essential meaning of references to it at Fatima, Lourdes and other places made holy by the presence of Mary in private revelations.

I commend this book to all who love God and our Blessed Mother; every reader will be enriched by a deeper understanding of the purposes and value of the Rosary.

+ Joseph A. Ferrario
Bishop of Honolulu

History of the Rosary

There is much academic controversy on the origin of the Rosary. We live in an era in which nearly everything must be confirmed by written evidence. The problem with this is that it is relatively recently in the history of mankind that the printed word has been with us. Prior to printing, much of what was believed had been passed on by word of mouth. People relied heavily on memory, and memory was acutely developed so that considerable information could be stored by the average individual. Some who were especially gifted could store vast amounts of information which was systematically told to others, who in turn related it to still others. This was the common means of passing on Christian prayers, devotions, stories of saints and various traditions.

In ancient and medieval days, few were well edu-
cated. Monasteries were often the centers of intellectual
endeavor and repositories of the written word. Catholic
universities also became centers of learning, but for the
few, not the masses.

Today we live in an age of sophisticated tools that
allow us to store and reference vast amounts of information. To apply today's standards to a great part of our
history would result in much not being verifiable. Some
propose that if we cannot verify information by current
strict standards of proof, then it should be discarded. But
if we do this, we will lose much of what may be true and
valuable.

The history of the Rosary can be viewed in this
context. For hundreds of years it was believed that the
Rosary was revealed to Spanish-born St. Dominic in the
early 13th century when he appealed to the Blessed
Virgin Mary to assist him in fighting the Albigensian
heresy. This has been a tradition of the Order of
Preachers (Dominicans) and passionately defended by its
members.

"You will know them by their fruits." Whether we
can prove historically that St. Dominic received this reve-
lation is not as important as the fact that the Dominicans
have zealously spread the use of the Rosary throughout
the world. They have been defenders and promoters of
the Rosary for centuries. This certainly suggests that
there must have been a basis in truth which led the Order
of Preachers to treasure and teach this devotion for so
long.

This leads to basic questions: Is the Rosary something good? Is it meant for this age, or was it for the past
alone? Is it only for the devout unlearned, or can it be

used by all to achieve the highest state of contemplation? Catholics are not required by Church law or divine command to believe in private revelations, even though they may have been approved as worthy of belief by the Church, and even though the Church has canonized those who were recipients of revelations. This is important to keep in mind even as we list here three well-known, Church-approved private revelations pertaining to the Rosary:

La Salette: In 1846, at La Salette in the French Alps, Mary the Mother of God instructed two children, Melanie Mathieu and Maximin Geraud on the constant necessity of prayer.

Lourdes: In 1854, the Blessed Virgin Mary appeared at Lourdes in France to a young girl, Bernadette Soubirous. The Virgin held a shining rosary. Our Holy Mother actually fingered her rosary as Bernadette said the prayers. She did so in silence except during the *Glory be,* when she joined Bernadette and spoke in praise of the Holy Trinity.

Fatima: Our Lady's approval of the Rosary at Lourdes became a positive command in the Fatima visions of 1917 in Portugal. She appeared to three shepherd children, Lucia dos Santos and her two cousins, Francisco and Jacinta Marto, each month from May to October. In each vision she asked that the Rosary be said every day.

The use of strings of beads or similar devices for aiding the memory and keeping count is pre-Christian. Monks of the Eastern Church use such a device of ancient origin, having one hundred or more beads with a different organization and entirely independent of the Western devotion. The custom of praying a number of

Our Father's or Hail Mary's (often 150, corresponding to the number of the Psalms in the Bible), and keeping count of them by means of a string of beads, was widespread in the West before the 13th century. There is also little doubt that the beads were used first for the counting of Our Father's.

The origin of the Rosary, as we know it today, can be traced back to ninth-century Ireland. In those days, the 150 Psalms were among the most important of monastic prayers and were recited or chanted daily.

Lay people who lived near the monasteries could discern the beauty of this devotion, but because very few people, other than the monks, knew how to read in those days—and the 150 Psalms are too long to memorize—such a form of prayer did not have popular application.

Around the year 800, a monk invited lay people to pray 150 Our Father's, since they could not pray the Psalms. This was the beginning of the development of the Rosary as we know it today.

The clergy and lay people in other parts of Europe began to recite the Angelic Salutation: "Hail Mary, full of grace, the Lord is with you. Blessed are you among women...." St. Peter Damian, who died in 1072, was the first to mention this prayer form.

The earliest known way of counting the 150 Our Father's was by discarding pebbles carried in a pouch. Each time an Our Father was said, a pebble would be discarded until all 150 pebbles were gone. Soon people devised cords with 150 or 50 knots. Later, strings with wooden beads came into use.

In the 13th century and throughout the Middle Ages, such articles were called *paternosters* ("*Pater Nos-*

ter" is "Our Father" in Latin), and those who made them were *paternosters*. In London, they worked in a street which is still called Paternoster Row.

During the 13th century another prayer form developed which gave the Rosary its mysteries. Medieval theologians had considered the 150 Psalms to be hidden prophecies of the life, death and resurrection of Jesus. With deep meditation and skillful interpretations, they began to compose "Psalters of Our Lord and Savior Jesus Christ." Each of the 150 Psalms was interpreted with reference to Jesus.

It was a natural development that 150 praises of Mary were soon composed as well. A shorter psalter of 50 Marian praises was often called a *rosarium* or bouquet.

There were a number of psalters in use during the 13th century: the 150 Our Father's, the 150 Angelic Salutations, the 150 praises of Jesus, and the 150 praises of Mary.

The year 1365 saw the first step toward combining these four kinds of psalters. Henry Kalkar, a Carthusian, divided the 150 Hail Mary's into groups of 10 and placed an Our Father between each of these decades.

In a book written around 1409 by Dominic the Prussian, 50 thoughts about the lives of Jesus and Mary were attached to a Rosary of 50 Hail Mary's.

Eventually, the 50 Hail Mary thoughts of Dominic the Prussian were divided into groups of 10, with an Our Father in between. From 1425 to 1470 many variations of this form were composed, with gradual changes.

A Dominican, Blessed Alan de la Roche, reportedly had founded the first Rosary confraternity by 1470, although many early writers attributed this to St. Dominic.

It is clear, however, that the missionary zeal of the Dominican Order can be traced from this period. Blessed Alan favored the Rosary form which had a special thought for each Hail Mary, which he called the "new" Rosary, while the form with no accompanying statements he called the "old" Rosary.

Through the efforts of Blessed Alan and the early Dominicans, the Rosary with 150 Hail Mary's, with a special thought for each bead, spread rapidly throughout the Western Christian world. Blessed Alan promoted this Rosary as the Rosary of St. Dominic.

As the Christian world moved out of the Middle Ages into the Renaissance period, the Rosary form with a thought for each Hail Mary was gradually abandoned. This came about because it was possible around 1500 to reproduce woodcut picture prints inexpensively for the first time. The picture Rosaries became immediately popular because the vast majority of people could not read. However, since it was difficult and expensive to draw and print 150 pictures for each Hail Mary thought, one picture was produced for every group of 10 beads, which was called a decade.

There were many variations introduced to stimulate meditation, usually in the form of narratives or meditations to be read before each decade.

The Popes and the Rosary

Throughout history the Popes have supported and promoted our Holy Mother's Rosary. They speak from the Chair of Peter to guide the flock to its Savior. We offer their words to give fresh encouragement to those who are devoted to this prayer; and to positively influence others who have either grown lukewarm and no longer pray this Marian prayer or are not familiar with it, that they may be moved by those who have occupied and do occupy the Chair of Peter.

St. Pius V wrote:

"...In times similar to our own, St. Dominic...was the founder of the Order of Friars Preachers, an institute to which we formerly belonged and whose Rule we expressly professed.

"The Albigensian heresy, then raging in part of France, had blinded so many of the laity that they were cruelly attacking priests and clerics. Blessed Dominic lifted his eyes to heaven and turned them toward that eminence, the Virgin Mary, the Mother of God, who alone had destroyed all heresies, and by the fruit of her womb crushed the head of the wily serpent and saved the world condemned by the sin of our first father. She is the woman from whom that rock was taken without the intervention of man, and this rock, struck by the wood, became the source of a torrent of graces. Dominic invented this method of prayer, which is easy and suitable to everyone, and which is called the Rosary or the Psalter of the Blessed Virgin Mary. It consists of venerating this Blessed Virgin by reciting 150 Angelic Salutations—the same number as the Psalms of David—interrupting them at each decade by the Lord's Prayer, meanwhile meditating on the mysteries which recall the entire life of our Lord Jesus Christ.

"After having devised it, Dominic and his sons spread this form of prayer throughout the Church. The faithful welcomed it with fervor, were soon set on fire by this meditation and were transformed into other men; the darkness of heresy receded; the light of the faith reappeared, and the Friars of the same Order, legitimately commissioned by their Superiors, founded associations of the Rosary everywhere, in which the faithful had themselves enrolled.

"Seeing this, the Church Militant which is entrusted to us, agitated at the present time by so many heresies and so horribly wounded and afflicted by wars and the depravity of morals, and following the example of our predecessors, we too now lift our eyes filled with tears, but also with hope, toward that summit from which comes all help, and we earnestly urge, in the Lord, all the faithful to imitate us. And to more easily encourage all to adopt this mode of prayer with devotion, respect and Christian sincerity, we use our authority definitely to approve and to confirm the validity and inviolable stability (of all the privileges granted to the association of the Rosary and to its members by our predecessors)."

On October 7, 1570, the Christian navy, although greatly outnumbered, scored a great victory over the Turkish navy at Lepanto. This victory prevented Turkish forces from overrunning Europe. While the battle was going on, the Confraternities of the Most Holy Rosary were continuously praying the Rosary, imploring God to grant them victory. On the day of the victory, the Holy Father had a premonition of this success, and attributed it to the Rosary prayers. In those days there were no modern methods of communication, and the news later confirmed the Pope's premonition. After the victory at Lepanto, St. Pius V changed the feast of the Blessed Virgin Mary of the Rosary to the day of the victory: "The day of the feast of the Blessed Virgin Mary of the Rosary ...from now on should be celebrated each year on October 7, instead of on the Second Sunday of May,...in memory of the victory of which we have spoken above and in honor of the Blessed Virgin...."

St. Pius V not only attributed to the Rosary the victory at Lepanto, but also noted its efficacy as a bulwark against heresies as well as armed attacks against Christianity. Beyond such capabilities he saw it also as a source of grace. He considered this prayer said in common by the Confraternities of the Rosary particularly powerful.

Pope Clement XIII reiterated the Rosary's power against heresies and granted a plenary indulgence in an Apostolic Letter *Ad Augendam,* as follows:

"We are moved by a deep love to dispose of the Church's heavenly treasures in order to increase the piety of the faithful and promote the salvation of souls. We, therefore, mercifully grant in the Lord a plenary indulgence, once a year, with the remission of all their sins, to each and every one of the faithful who, being truly repentant, having confessed their sins and strengthened themselves with Holy Communion, devoutly recite the Rosary of the Most Blessed Virgin Mary at the hour assigned to them, and pray for harmony among Christian princes, for the extirpation of heresies, and for the exultation of our Holy Mother the Church. They may apply this indulgence by way of suffrage to the souls of the faithful who have left this life in a state of union with God in charity."

Pope Pius IX saw the Rosary as a way of obtaining the assistance of the Immaculate Mother of God in the Church's fight against heresies and vices:

"After St. Dominic had founded the Order of Preachers, it was his desire to put an end to the errors of the Albigensians. Moved by divine inspiration, he began to implore the help of the Immaculate Mother of God, to whom alone it has been given to wipe out all the heresies in the universe, and he preached the Rosary as an infallible protection against heresies and vices....

"...'The Perpetual Rosary,' [was] founded in Bologna at the beginning of the 17th century, thanks to the zeal of the members of the Order of Friars Preachers, as was reported to us. Every member was to take his turn reciting the Rosary at the different hours of the day and night as a perpetual homage addressed to the Mother of God.

"...Therefore we, after God, have placed all our confidence in the Blessed Virgin Mary. We are comforted by the hope that, thanks to the frequent recitation of the Rosary everywhere by the faithful, she will destroy, as in times past, the monstrous errors which are being spread today, and she will put an end to the criminal activities of the impious....

"This devotion, which reverently honors both the principal mysteries of Christ and her who alone has crushed every heresy of the 13th century and later on, often defeated the enemies of the Church. Rightly, therefore, we must hope that the same power will repulse the errors of hell, will annihilate the machinations of godlessness, will remove from the people the errors that have been propagated and, with it, the great upheaval that convulses all mankind."

Pope Leo XIII was greatly devoted to our Holy Mother and was a promoter of the Rosary. He called the Blessed Virgin Mary the "Mediatrix of our peace with God and the Dispenser of heavenly graces," and exhorted:

"The solemn anniversaries that recall to mind the numerous and substantial blessings that devotion to the holy Rosary has won for the Christian people are at hand. It is our wish that these prayers be offered this year with special fervor to the Blessed Virgin, so that through her intercession we may obtain from her Son a favorable alleviation and an end to our evils.

"...The Blessed Virgin was exempt from the stain of original sin and chosen to be the Mother of God. For this very reason she was associated with him in the work of man's salvation, and enjoys favor and power with her Son greater than any human or angel has ever attained or could attain.

"And since Mary's greatest joy is to grant her help and assistance to those who call upon her, there is no reason to doubt that she wishes not only to answer the prayers of the universal Church, but that she is eager to do so.

"This great and confident devotion to the august Queen of Heaven has shone forth more brightly whenever the militant Church of God was endangered by the violence of widespread heresy, by the spread of moral corruption, or by the attacks of powerful enemies. Ancient and modern history and the more sacred annals of the Church bear witness to the public and private supplications addressed to the Mother of God, to the help she has granted in return, and to the public peace and tranquillity which she has obtained from God.

"Rightly, therefore, she has been hailed as 'Help of Christians,' 'Consolation of the Afflicted,' 'Queen of Armies,' 'Queen of Victory and Peace.' But of all the titles, that of the *'Queen of the Rosary'* (emphasis added) is especially noteworthy and solemn. Through it singular blessings for which Christians are indebted to her have been forever hallowed.''

Succeeding Leo XIII was *St. Pius X*, also a supporter of the Rosary and of organizations formed to pray the Rosary in groups. In 1908, he wrote the following to the head of the Perpetual Rosary Association:

"There is nothing more excellent it seems to us, than that numerous voices are uninterruptingly and from many parts of the world simultaneously lifting up supplications to the Blessed Virgin Mary as they meditate on the Christian mysteries, so that the blessings of her maternal goodness may not cease to descend upon the Church. We, therefore, rejoice that we have the opportunity to make known our benevolence and our love...."

Pope John XXIII, who convened the Second Vatican Council, had a great love for the Rosary. He wrote:

"As an exercise of Christian devotion among the faithful of the Latin Rite who constitute a notable portion of the Catholic family, *the Rosary ranks after Holy Mass and the Breviary for ecclesiastics, and for the laity after participation in the sacraments.* (Emphasis added.) It is a devout form of union with God and lifts souls to a high supernatural plane.

"...The true substance of the well-meditated Rosary consists in a threefold element that gives unity and cohesion to the vocal expression, unfolding in vivid succession the episodes which join together the life of Jesus and Mary, in reference to the different conditions of the persons praying and to the aspirations of the universal Church.

"For each decade of Hail Mary's there is a picture, and for each picture a *threefold emphasis* which is simultaneously: *mystical contemplation, intimate reflection and pious intention.*

Mystical Contemplation

"First of all there is a pure, luminous and brief contemplation of each mystery, that is, of those truths of the faith which speak to us of the redemptive mission of Jesus. By contemplating we find ourselves in an intimate communication of thought and sentiment with the teaching and life of Jesus, Son of God and Son of Mary, who lived on earth to redeem, to teach and to sanctify—in the silence of his hidden life of prayer and work, in the sufferings of his blessed passion, in the triumph of his resurrection, as well as his heavenly glory where he sits at the right hand of the Father, always active in assisting and vivifying through the Holy Spirit the Church which he founded and which is progressing in its journey through the centuries.

Intimate Reflection

"The second element is reflection, which diffuses itself in clear light from the fullness of the mysteries of Christ over the spirit of the person praying. Each person sees in the single mysteries the timely and good teaching as it concerns him, his own sanctification and the particular circumstances of his life. Under the continuous enlightenment of the Holy Spirit, who from the depths of the soul in the state of grace 'makes intercession for us with groanings that cannot be expressed in speech' (Romans 8:26), each one confronts his life with the warmth of the teaching which springs from those same mysteries, and he finds countless applications in them for his own spiritual needs as well as for those of his daily life.

Pious Intention

"The last element is *intention*, that is, the singling out of persons, institutions or needs of a personal or social order, which for a truly active and pious Catholic constitute the objects of his brotherly love, a love which is diffused in hearts as the living expression of common membership in the Mystical Body of Christ.

Universal Prayer

"In this manner the Rosary becomes the universal prayer of everyone and of the vast community of the Redeemer, who meet together in a single prayer from every corner of the world, whether it be in personal prayer, imploring graces for their individual needs, or whether it be in the participation in the immense and unanimous choir of all the Church in intercession for all mankind....

Everyone's Prayer

"Oh! How beautiful is the Rosary of the innocent child and of those who are sick, of the consecrated virgin in the seclusion of the cloister or in the humble and self-sacrificing apostolate of charity; of the man and woman, father and mother of a family, imbued with an exalted and Christian responsibility; of humble families faithful to the ancient tradition of the home....

Public and Universal Prayer

"While respecting this ancient, customary and moving form of Marian devotion as applied to each one's particular circumstances, we may also add that the modern transformations which have arisen in every sector of human life awaken new feelings even about the functions and forms of Christian prayer.... Henceforth everyone who prays no longer feels himself alone and occupied exclusively with his own spiritual and temporal interests. He realizes, more clearly than in the past, that he belongs to a whole social body, shares in its responsibilities, enjoys its benefits, and fears for its uncertainties and dangers....

"Mary's Rosary is thus raised to the height of a great public and universal prayer for all the ordinary and extraordinary needs of Holy Church, of nations and of the entire world...."

The Holy Father himself gave an example of devotion to the Rosary.

"When you return to your homes, bring our greeting to your dear ones: tell them also that the Pope recites the entire Rosary, that is, the fifteen decades every day...."

Pope Paul VI, who presided over the Second Vatican Council after Pope John XXIII had passed away, wrote his Apostolic Exhortation *Marialis Cultus* in 1974, and wrote and talked about our Holy Mother constantly. He who guided Vatican II to its culmination asked children to pray the Rosary for the success of the Council. He also indicated that the Vatican Council supported the praying of the Rosary: "The Second Vatican Council recommended the use of the Rosary to all the sons of the Church, not in express words but in unmistakable fashion in this sentence: 'Let them value highly the pious practices and exercises directed to the Blessed Virgin and approved over the centuries by the magisterium.'" He pointed out: "It is by now a tradition for the Popes of these last centuries to offer an ever renewed and special homage to our Lady through the explanation, defense and recommendation of the holy Rosary.... It is easy to understand the reasons for so great a pontifical devotion to our Lady. No one is as devoted to Mary most holy as the Pope!"

Paul VI frequently quoted Pope Leo XIII as a great promoter and defender of Mary and her holy Rosary:

"Permit us to repeat only those words which Leo XIII quoted in his Encyclical *Adiutricem Populi,* taking them from the lips of St. Cyril of Alexandria. The latter was the principal promoter of the Council of Ephesus, where Mary was recognized and proclaimed to be the Mother of God. He addressed her in these words: 'Through you [Mary], the apostles preached salvation to the nations; through you the precious cross is extolled and adored through the entire world; through you the demons are put to flight and people are called back to heaven; through you every creature, held fast by the error of idolatry, has come to the knowledge of truth; through you the faithful have received holy Baptism, and churches have been built throughout the world.'

"These are words that instill in us confidence in the most holy Virgin.... For us, they allow us to hope that the Council will have a happy outcome and that souls will come closer to Christ, at a time when they take the Rosary in their hands once again with a great desire, with a new resolve to begin again the delightful rhythm: *Ave Maria, Ave Maria.*"

Pope John Paul II has dedicated his pontificate to the Blessed Virgin Mary. He has often exhorted the faithful to seek the intercession of Mary, and there is hardly a talk or a sermon that does not allude to Mary. The Pope's statements on the Rosary have yet to be fully documented, but there is enough already to show the Holy Father's devotion to this prayer:

"The Rosary is my favorite prayer. A marvelous prayer! Marvelous in its simplicity and in its depth.... It can be said that the Rosary is, in a certain way, a prayer-commentary on the last chapter of the Constitution *Lu-*

men *Gentium* of Vatican II, a chapter which deals with the wonderful presence of the Mother of God in the mystery of Christ and the Church.

"In fact, against the background of the words *Ave Maria* there pass before the eyes of the soul the main episodes in the life of Jesus Christ.... They put us in living communion with Jesus through—we could say—his Mother's heart.

"At the same time our heart can enclose in these decades of the Rosary all the facts that make up the life of the individual, the family, the nation, the Church, and mankind. Personal matters and those of one's neighbor, and particularly of those who are closest to us, who are dearest to us. Thus, in the simple prayer of the Rosary beats the rhythm of human life.

"During the last few weeks I have had the opportunity to meet many persons, representatives of various nations and of different environments as well as of various Christian churches and communities. I wish to assure you that I have not failed to translate these relations into the language of the Rosary prayer, that everyone might find himself at the heart of the prayer which gives a full dimension to everything."

Before it gets too late in the day, the Holy Father gathers his household together for the recitation of the Rosary. He also gives rosaries to those to whom he grants audiences. And he leads the Rosary on Vatican Radio the first Saturday of each month.

"It is Mary," he has said, "who will help us to find time for prayer. Through the Rosary, that great gospel prayer, she will help us to know Christ. We need to live as she did, in the presence of God, raising our minds and hearts to him in our daily activities and worries."

Through the Rosary, the Holy Father thanks the Lord that he recovered from an assassin's attempt on his life. "It was 'thanks to the Lord that I was not destroyed.' I said it for the first time on the occasion of the feast of the Virgin of the Rosary. I repeat it today at Fatima, which speaks to us so much of the Rosary—the recitation of the third part of the Rosary—as the little shepherds said. The Rosary, its third part, is and will always remain a prayer of gratitude, of love and faithful entreaty—the prayer of the Mother of the Church!

Apparitions and the Rosary

This book has its emphasis on the Rosary, and while we are tempted to treat in greater depth the apparitions of our Lady, it would detract from our major purpose. The Rosary is not an end in itself but a means to an end—namely, to assist in the salvation of our souls and the souls of others. The apparitions of our Lady have a more specific but related purpose or message. Usually the message is basically the same—repent, renew your lives, pray, reconsecrate your hearts to God with and through Mary. This, of course, does not do justice to the nuances of apparitions as, for example, at Lourdes, when our holy Mother informed Bernadette, after repeated requests, that she, Mary, is the Immaculate Conception; or at Fatima, when our holy Mother informed Lucia that Jesus desires devotion to her Immaculate Heart.

We repeat what we said earlier, that the Church—even though it approves certain apparitions—does not require belief in them. We have already mentioned the apparitions at La Salette and Lourdes. We see them as stepping-stones to Fatima as it pertains to the Rosary. We refer again to La Salette and Lourdes, and will dwell longer on Fatima.

La Salette

On September 19, 1846, our holy Mother appeared to Melanie Mathieu, a girl fifteen years old, and Maximin Geraud, a boy of eleven, as they were tending cows on a high mountainous plateau in Southeastern France. The children saw a luminous globe which seemed to divide, and then they saw a Lady seated on a large rock. She had her face in her hands, and she was weeping bitterly. The two children were frightened, but when the tall, beautiful, stately Lady stood up, crossed her arms, and called them to her, telling them not to be frightened, they were no longer afraid. The Lady had on a long white dress with a golden apron tied at the waist. Her white shawl was bordered with roses of different colors. Her white shoes were bordered with the same many-colored roses. Around her neck hung a chain with a crucifix. On the crossbar of the crucifix were affixed a hammer and pincers. A crown of roses radiated bright rays like a diadem. In the Lady's beautiful eyes were tears which then ran down her cheeks. There was a brilliance of light which surrounded her, brighter than the sun, but different.

She told the children that the hand of her Son was so

strong and heavy that she could no longer hold it back, and that unless people did penance and obeyed God's law they would have much to suffer. She predicted a terrible famine, and confided to each child a secret which they revealed to no one—except later to the Pope, at his request.

She asked the children whether they said their prayers well. When they answered "not very well," she told them to *say them carefully* every morning and every night—never to say less than *an Our Father and a Hail Mary.*

Pope Pius IX approved the devotion to Our Lady of La Salette. He asked the children to write down the secrets and send them to him. He later said: "These are the secrets of La Salette. Unless the world repents, it shall perish!"

Lourdes

On February 11, 1858, Bernadette, her sister Toinette and one of her neighbors, Jeanne Abadie, started off at about noon to look for firewood along the banks of the Gave River in France. They passed a cliff called Massabielle in which nature had hollowed out a grotto. Bernadette, who was asthmatic, did not immediately cross the shallow stream in front of the grotto with the other girls. She heard a sound like a strong gust of wind. Looking in the direction of the grotto, she was startled by the sight of a beautiful Lady in white standing there. Grabbing her rosary out of her pocket, she tried to make the Sign of the Cross but found that she could not lift her arm. She was paralyzed with fear and amazement.

The Lady smiled sweetly, took her own shining ro-

*sary and made the Sign of the Cross. This time Berna-
dette succeeded in making the Sign of the Cross, fell to
her knees and prayed the Rosary in the presence of the
beautiful Lady. While Bernadette prayed, the Lady fingered her rosary in silence, except during the Glory be,
when she joined Bernadette.*

The following Sunday Bernadette was drawn to the
grotto, and received her mother's permission to go there
with some companions as long as they brought holy
water with them. They had just begun the Rosary when
the Lady appeared to Bernadette who, as her mother had
instructed her, sprinkled holy water three times in the
direction of the vision. She told the Lady to come for-
ward if she were a messenger of God. With a smile the
Lady advanced toward Bernadette. *Bernadette finished
the Rosary with her companions and became so enrap-
tured with her beautiful Lady that she was unaware of
what was going on around her.*

The following Thursday our Lady again appeared to
Bernadette at the grotto and asked her to return every day
for two weeks. Our Lady appeared to Bernadette eighteen
times. As can be imagined, this caused quite a furor, and
Bernadette was besieged by questions. She gave the same
answer, ''She is a beautiful Lady—she is kind—*she car-
ries a rosary.''*

Our Lady revealed secrets to Bernadette. She asked
for prayers for poor sinners, pleaded for sacrifice and
penance, and showed Bernadette the miraculous spring
whose waters would cure many souls and bodies. The
Lady asked for a chapel to be built at the grotto.

The parish pastor insisted that the Lady indicate
who she was. On March 25, 1858, after Bernadette asked

her three times to give her name, the beautiful Lady said, "I am the Immaculate Conception."

It was a dogma which Pope Pius IX had proclaimed some four years earlier on December 8, 1854. Bernadette knew nothing of this. It was our Lady's way of confirming the dogma that from the first moment of her conception she was preserved free from the stain of original sin.

The final apparition occurred on July 16, the Feast of Our Lady of Mount Carmel. Bernadette said that our Lady seemed more beautiful than ever.

Hundreds of thousands of people now visit Lourdes every year, and Lourdes water has been spread throughout the world. The pilgrims join in the midnight candlelight procession, *praying the Rosary* and singing the "Ave Maria" hymn. Many miracles—bodily cures—have been recorded. Many healings of souls have not been officially recorded but are believed to have occurred.

In 1846, before the dogma was officially declared by the Holy See, the Bishops of the United States consecrated the nation to the Immaculate Conception. Mary is the patroness of the United States under that title.

Fatima

As we have seen, our holy Mother appears to simple, humble hearts. These are usually the uncluttered hearts of children. Bernadette Soubirous was fourteen years old. Maximin Giraud was eleven, and Melanie Mathieu was fifteen. Juan Diego, to whom Our Lady of Guadalupe appeared in December, 1531, was a poor, simple, good and kind Aztec Indian.

St. Therese of Lisieux has shown us that we must be childlike before God, our Maker and Sustainer.

Fatima was no different. Our holy Mother appeared to three shepherd children in 1917: Lucia dos Santos, age ten, and her cousins, Francisco, eight, and Jacinta Marto, six.

Prior to the visions of our Lady in 1917, the children were visited by an angel who called himself the Angel of Peace and the Angel of Portugal. He was, it appeared, paving the way for the Queen of Angels and of humanity.

In each of her apparitions our Lady asked that the Rosary be prayed.

Much has been written of Our Lady of Fatima. In particular, William Thomas Walsh was instrumental in informing Americans of Our Lady of Fatima through his book by that name, published by the Macmillan Company in 1947.

We have chosen to quote the memoirs of Lucia, since she was one of the seers and, in fact, the spokesperson for the children with our holy Mother. Lucia uses words sparingly. She is still living, an elderly Carmelite nun— Sr. Mary of the Sorrows—following the quiet, cloistered, prayerful life of the Carmelite Order.

In 1915, Lucia saw three apparitions of what she judged later to be the angel. The apparitions "appeared to be a cloud in human form, whiter than snow and almost transparent."

The angel did not speak as he later did in 1916.

"...I think it must have been in the spring of 1916 that the angel appeared to us for the first time in our Loca do Cabeco.... We had climbed the hill in search of shelter. After taking our lunch and saying our prayers, we began to see, some distance off, above the trees that stretched away towards the east, a light, whiter than snow, in the form of a young man, transparent, and brighter than crystal pierced by the rays of the sun. As he drew nearer, we could distinguish his features more and more clearly. We were surprised, absorbed and struck dumb with amazement.''

When he reached Lucia, Jacinta and Francisco he said: "Do not be afraid. I am the Angel of Peace. Pray with me."

"Kneeling on the ground, he bowed down until his forehead touched the earth. Led by a supernatural impulse, we did the same, and repeated the words which we heard him say: 'My God, I believe, I adore, I hope and I love you! I ask pardon of you for those who do not believe, do not adore, do not hope and do not love you.'

"Having repeated these words three times, he rose and said: 'Pray thus. The Hearts of Jesus and Mary are attentive to the voice of your supplications.' Then he disappeared.

"The supernatural atmosphere which enveloped us was so intense that we were for a long time scarcely aware of our own existence, remaining in the same posture in which he had left us, and continually repeating the same prayer....

"The second apparition must have been at the height of summer, when the heat of the day was so intense that we had to take the sheep home before noon and only let them out again in the early evening.

"We went to spend the siesta hours in the shade of the trees which surrounded the well.... Suddenly we saw the same angel right beside us.

"'What are you doing?' he asked. 'Pray. Pray very much! The Hearts of Jesus and Mary have designs of mercy on you. Offer prayers and sacrifices constantly to the Most High.'

" 'How are we to make sacrifices?' I asked.

" 'Make a sacrifice of everything you can, and offer it to God as an act of reparation for the sins by which he is offended, and in supplication for the conversion of sinners. You will thus draw peace upon your country. I am its Angel Guardian, the Angel of Portugal. Above all, accept and bear with submission the suffering which the Lord will send you.'

"These words were indelibly impressed upon our minds. They were like a light which made us understand who God is, how he loves us and desires to be loved, the value of sacrifice and how pleasing it is to him, and how, on account of it, he grants the grace of conversion to sinners....

"It seems to me that the third apparition must have been in October, or towards the end of September, as we were no longer returning home for siesta.

"...We went one day from Pregueira (a small olive grove belonging to my parents) to the Lapa, making our way along the slope of the hill on the side facing Aljustrel and Casa Velha. We said our Rosary there and the prayer the angel had taught us at the first apparition.

"While we were there the angel appeared to us for the third time, holding a chalice in his hands, with a Host above it from which drops of blood were falling into the sacred vessel. Leaving the chalice and the Host suspended in the air, the angel prostrated himself on the ground and repeated this prayer three times:

" 'Most Holy Trinity—Father, Son and Holy Spirit, I adore you profoundly, and I offer you the most precious Body, Blood, Soul and Divinity of Jesus Christ, present in all the tabernacles of the world, in reparation for the outrages, sacrileges and indifference with which he himself is offended. And, through the infinite merits of his Most Sacred Heart, and the Immaculate Heart of Mary, I beg of you the conversion of poor sinners.'

"Then rising, he once more took the chalice and the Host in his hands. He gave the Host to me, and to Jacinta and Francisco he gave the contents of the chalice to drink, saying as he did so: 'Take and drink the Body and Blood of Jesus Christ, horribly outraged by ungrateful people. Repair their crimes and console your God,' and then he disappeared.

"Impelled by the power of the supernatural that enveloped us, we imitated all that the angel had done, prostrating ourselves on the ground as he did, and repeating the prayers that he had said. The force of the presence of God was so intense that it absorbed us and almost completely annihilated us.... The peace and happiness which we felt were great, but wholly interior, for our souls were completely immersed in God. The physical exhaustion that came over us was also great."

May 13, 1917

Our holy Mother first appeared to the children on May 13, 1917. The three little shepherds were again tending their sheep. Lucia's commentary continues:

"High up on the slope in the Cova da Iria, I was playing with Jacinta and Francisco at building a little stone wall around a clump of furze. Suddenly we saw what seemed to be a flash of lightning.

"'We'd better go home,' I said to my cousin. 'That's lightning; we may have a thunderstorm.'

"'Yes, indeed,' they answered.

"We began to go down the slope, hurrying the sheep along towards the road. We were more or less halfway down the slope, and almost level with a large holm oak tree that stood there, when we saw another flash of lightning. We had only gone a few steps farther when, there before us on a small holm oak, we beheld a Lady all dressed in white. She was more brilliant than the sun, and radiated a light more clear and intense than a crystal glass filled with sparkling water, when the rays of the sun shine through it.

"We stopped, astounded, before the apparition. We were so close, just a few feet from her, that we were bathed in the light which surrounded her, or rather, which radiated from her. Then our Lady spoke to us:

" 'Do not be afraid. I will do you no harm.'

"I asked, 'Where are you from?'

" 'I am from heaven.'

" 'What do you want of me?'

" 'I have come to ask you to come here for six months in succession, on the 13th day, at this same hour. Later on, I will tell you who I am and what I want. Afterwards, I will return here yet a seventh time. (The seventh time refers to June 16, 1921, which had a personal message for Lucia.)

" 'Shall I go to heaven too?' I asked.

" 'Yes, you will.'

" 'And Jacinta?'

" 'She will go also.'

" 'And Francisco?'

" 'He will go there too, *but he must say many Rosaries.*' (Emphasis added.)

"Then I remembered to ask about two girls who had died recently. They were friends of mine and used to come to my home to learn weaving with my eldest sister.

" 'Is Maria das Neves in heaven?'

" 'Yes, she is.' (I think she was about sixteen years old.)

" 'And Amelia?'

" 'She will be in purgatory until the end of the world.' (It seems to me she was between eighteen and twenty years of age.)

" 'Are you willing to offer yourselves to God and bear all the sufferings he wills to send to you, as an act of reparation for the sins by which he is offended, and of supplication for the conversion of sinners?'

" 'Yes, we are willing.'

" 'Then you are going to have much to suffer, but the grace of God will be your comfort.'

"As she pronounced these last words '...the grace of God will be your comfort,' our Lady opened her hands for the first time, communicating to us a light so intense that, as it streamed from her hands, its rays penetrated our hearts and the innermost depths of our souls, making us see ourselves in God, who was that light, more clearly than we see ourselves in the best of mirrors. Then, moved by an interior impulse that was also communicated to us, we fell to our knees, repeating in our hearts: 'O most Holy Trinity, I adore you! My God, my God, I love you in the most Blessed Sacrament!'

"After a few moments our Lady spoke again: '*Pray the Rosary every day, in order to obtain peace in the world, and the end of the war.*' (Emphasis added.)

"Then she began to rise serenely, going up towards the east, until she disappeared in the immensity of space. The light that surrounded her seemed to open a path before her in the firmament, and for this reason we sometimes said that we saw heaven opening."

In this first apparition our holy Mother referred to the Rosary twice. First in referring to Francisco that he too would go to heaven but "must say many Rosaries." We see then that the Rosary is a means of assisting us to gain heaven.

Secondly, our holy Mother said that we should "pray the Rosary every day in order to obtain peace in the world...." It is also then a means of obtaining peace and ending conflict. While our holy Mother was referring to the First World War, we may assume that she also means that it is a way to obtain peace in any conflict. In particular, to bring peace to the hearts of all, peace in the family, peace at the work place, peace not only between nations but within nations. It is a way to quiet conflict within the soul and to give the soul tranquillity.

June 13, 1917

On June 13, 1917, our holy Mother appeared to Lucia, Jacinta and Francisco for the second time, just as she had promised. Lucia continues her story:

"As soon as Jacinta, Francisco and I had finished praying the Rosary, with a number of other people who were present, we saw once more the flash reflecting the light which was approaching (this we called lightning). The next moment, our Lady was there on the holm oak, exactly the same as in May.

"'What do you want of me?' I asked.

"'I wish you to come here on the 13th of next month, *to pray the Rosary every day,* and to learn to read. (Emphasis added.) Later, I will tell you what I want.'

"I asked for the cure of a sick person.

" 'If he is converted, he will be cured during the year.'

" 'I would also like to ask you to take us to heaven.'

" 'Yes, I will take Jacinta and Francisco soon. But you are to stay here some time longer. Jesus wishes to make use of you to make me known and loved. He wants to establish in the world *devotion to my Immaculate Heart*.' (Emphasis added.)

" 'Am I to stay here alone?' I asked, sadly.

" 'No, my daughter. Are you suffering a great deal? Don't lose heart. I will never forsake you. My Immaculate Heart will be your refuge and the way that will lead you to God.'

"As our Lady spoke these last words, she opened her hands and for the second time, she communicated to us the rays of that same immense light. We saw ourselves in this light, as it were, immersed in God. Jacinta and Francisco seemed to be in that part of the light which rose towards heaven, and I in that which was poured out on the earth. In front of the palm of our Lady's right hand was a heart encircled by thorns which pierced it. We understood that this was the Immaculate Heart of Mary, outraged by the sins of humanity, and seeking reparation."

For the second time our holy Mother asked that the Rosary be prayed every day. In fact, during this second apparition she appeared right after the children and those who accompanied them had finished praying their Rosary. This time she did not indicate a purpose for praying it. (You will recall that in the first apparition she asked that the Rosary be prayed for peace and for the end of the war.)

Our holy Mother introduced a new subject—that Jesus her Son wants to establish devotion to her Immaculate Heart in the world. Our holy Mother used the language of the people, as her Son did while he was on earth. When she referred to her Immaculate Heart she meant her Immaculate Soul. We know that the heart is an organ that pumps life-giving blood throughout the body. Our holy Mother is referring to the "interior" of her Immaculate Soul, her motherly soul, which sends God's life-giving grace to her children.

July 13, 1917

The third apparition occurred on July 13, 1917, and by this time there was a large crowd gathered at the Cova da Iria. Lucia continues:

"A few minutes after arriving at the Cova da Iria, near the holm oak, where a large number of people were praying the Rosary, we saw the flash of light once more, and a moment later our Lady appeared on the holm oak.

" 'What do you want of me?' I asked.

" 'I want you to come here on the 13th of next month, *to continue to pray the Rosary every day in honor of Our Lady of the Rosary, in order to obtain peace for the world and the end of the war, because only she can help you.* (Emphasis added.)

" 'I would like to ask you to tell us who you are, and to work a miracle so that everybody will believe that you are appearing to us.'

" 'Continue to come here every month. In October, I will tell you who I am and what I want, and I will perform a miracle for all to see and believe.'

"I then made some requests, but I cannot recall now just what they were. What I do remember is that *our Lady said it was necessary for such people to pray the Rosary in order to obtain these graces during the year.* (Emphasis added.) And she continued:

" 'Sacrifice yourself for sinners, and say many times, especially whenever you make some sacrifice: O Jesus, it is for love of you, for the conversion of sinners, and in reparation for the sins committed against the Immaculate Heart of Mary.'

"As our Lady spoke these last words she opened her hands once more, as she had done on the two previous occasions. The rays of light seemed to penetrate the earth, and we saw, as it were, a sea of fire. Plunged into this fire were demons and souls in human form, like transparent burning embers, all blackened or burnished bronze, floating about in conflagration, now raised into the air by the flames that issued from within themselves together with great clouds of smoke, now falling back on every side like sparks in huge fires, without weight or equilibrium, amid shrieks and groans of pain and despair, which horrified us and made us tremble with fear. (It must have been this sight which caused me to cry out, as people say they heard me.) The demons could be distinguished by their terrifying and repellent likeness to frightful and unknown animals, black and transparent like burning coals. Terrified, and as if to plead for succor, we looked up at our Lady, who said to us, so kindly and so sadly:

" 'You have seen hell where the souls of poor sinners go. *To save them, God wishes to establish in the world devotion to my Immaculate Heart.* (Emphasis added.) If what I say to you is done, many souls will be saved and there will be peace. The war is going to end; but if people do not cease offending God, a worse one will break out during the pontificate of Pius XI. When you see a night illumined by an unknown light, know that this is the great sign given you by God that he is about to punish the world for its crimes, by means of war, famine, and persecutions of the Church and of the Holy Father.

"'To prevent this, I shall come to ask for the consecration of Russia to my Immaculate Heart, and the Communion of Reparation on the First Saturday. If my requests are heeded, Russia will be converted, and there will be peace; if not, she will spread her errors throughout the world, causing wars and persecutions of the Church. The good will be martyred, the Holy Father will have much to suffer, various nations will be annihilated. In the end, my Immaculate Heart will triumph. The Holy Father will consecrate Russia to me, and she will be converted, and a period of peace will be granted to the world....

"'When you pray the Rosary, say after each mystery: O my Jesus, forgive us, save us from the fire of hell. Lead all souls to heaven, especially those who are most in need.' (Emphasis added.)

"'Is there anything more that you want of me?'

"'No, I do not want anything more of you today.'

"Then, as before, our Lady began to ascend toward the east, until she finally disappeared in the immense distance of the firmament."

In this third apparition our Lady had more to say than in any of the others. She referred to the Rosary three times. She asked that the Rosary be prayed in honor of Our Lady of the Rosary. This prayer is so close to her heart, so much a part of her, that she refers to herself by that title. Again she said that the Rosary is to be prayed to obtain peace in the world and an end to the war.

She showed the children a vision of hell, and said that in order to save poor sinners God wished to establish devotion to her Immaculate Heart. She warned that if people didn't cease offending God, a worse war would break out during the pontificate of Pius XI. This indeed did happen with World War II.

She asked that Russia be consecrated to her Immaculate Heart and that the Communion of Reparation be established on the first Saturdays of the month. Lucia reports a later vision of December 10, 1925, at which time our holy Mother further explained the Communion of Reparation:

"...I promise to assist at the hour of death, with the graces necessary for salvation, all those who, on the first Saturday of five consecutive months, shall confess, receive Holy Communion and *recite five decades of the Rosary* (emphasis added), with the intention of making reparation to me."

In a vision on February 15, 1926, Jesus explained to Lucia that confession need not be made on the Saturday, if there is difficulty, but that it could be eight days or even farther distant from the first Saturday, "...provided that when they receive me, they are in a state of grace and have the intention of making reparation to the Immaculate Heart of Mary."

In the apparition of July 13, 1917, our holy Mother also said that for the people to obtain the requests they made, it was necessary to "pray the Rosary." She also requested that the "O my Jesus..." prayer be said after each decade of the Rosary.

August 19, 1917

The children were detained by the civil authorities, and in fact were jailed, so they could not go to the Cova da Iria on August 13. On August 19, 1917, the fourth apparition occurred. Lucia continues her story in her memoirs:

"I was accompanied by Francisco and his brother John. We were with the sheep in a place called Valinhos, when we felt something supernatural approaching and enveloping us. Suspecting that our Lady was about to appear to us, and feeling sorry because Jacinta might miss seeing her, we asked her brother to go and call her. As he was unwilling to go, I offered him two small coins, and off he ran.

"Meanwhile, Francisco and I saw the flash of light which we called lightning. Jacinta arrived and a moment later, we saw our Lady on a holm oak tree.

" 'What do you want of me?'

" *'I want you to continue praying the Rosary every day.* (Emphasis added.) In the last month, I will perform a miracle so that all may believe.'

" 'What do you want done with the money that the people leave in the Cova da Iria?'

" 'Have two litters made. One is to be carried by you and Jacinta and two other girls dressed in white; the other one is to be carried by Francisco and three other boys. The money from the litters is for the *Feast of Our Lady of the Rosary,* and what is left over will help towards the construction of a chapel that is to be built here.' (Emphasis added.)

" 'I would like to ask you to cure some sick persons.'

" 'Yes, I will cure some of them during the year.' Then looking very sad, our Lady said:

" 'Pray, pray very much, and make sacrifices for sinners; for many souls go to hell, because there are none to sacrifice themselves and to pray for them.'

"And she began to ascend as usual to the east."

As in the other apparitions, our holy Mother asked that the Rosary be prayed every day. She also referred to the Feast of Our Lady of the Rosary. "Pray very much and make sacrifices for sinners" to save them from hell, admonished our Mother. It seems as if she was almost begging for prayer and sacrifice to save souls. She is the Mother of all people—all are her children. Can we imagine the sorrow of that Immaculate Heart when any of her children are lost to hell? It is clear that the Rosary is important in this battle for souls. It is also clear that although God is almighty, he has so set the forces of justice that our cooperation is needed for our own salvation and the salvation of others. We must make up in our own bodies what is lacking in the suffering of Christ. Not that there is anything truly lacking in the purity, sincerity, extent and value of our Lord's suffering. It is just that as his holy Mother cooperates so well in the salvation of man, so he has willed that we, as his brothers and sisters, be one with him in this salvific effort.

September 13, 1917

The fifth apparition, on September 13, 1917, was the briefest. There were thousands of people, many of them shouting their intentions at the children so that Lucia might pass them on to our holy Mother.

"At last, we arrived at the Cova da Iria, and on reaching the holm oak we began to say the Rosary with the people. Shortly afterwards, we saw the flash of light, and then our Lady appeared on the holm oak.

" '*Continue to pray the Rosary in order to obtain the end of the war.* (Emphasis added.) In October our Lord will come as well as Our Lady of Sorrows and Our Lady of Carmel. St. Joseph will appear with the Child Jesus to bless the world. God is pleased with your sacrifices.'

" 'I was told to ask you many things, the cure of some sick people, a deaf mute....'

" 'Yes, I will cure some, but not others. In October, I will perform a miracle so that all may believe.'

"Then our Lady began to rise as usual, and disappeared."

For the fifth consecutive time our holy Mother asked that the Rosary be prayed. The question to be asked is whether the Blessed Virgin meant that the Rosary be prayed only during that time and by those people or whether it is meant as a universal prayer for all times. Is it meant only for children or for adults as well? Is it meant for uneducated people or for the learned as well? We have already alluded to these questions. We pose them again here, for it is clear that if one chooses to believe in these Church-approved apparitions, our holy Mother does not place restrictions on this prayer with regard to time, place or degree of education. The Queen of the universe clearly wants her Rosary universally prayed in all ages.

October 13, 1917

Despite a severe rainstorm, thousands of people trudged through mud on the evening of October 12 to sleep outdoors in order to be in a good position on October 13. Men and women moved through the mud on their knees, recited the Rosary and sang songs together.

On the 13th of October there were some 70,000 people of all ages and conditions waiting patiently for the children and for the promised miracle.

Lucia relates what took place:

"On the way, scenes of the previous month, still more numerous and moving, were repeated. Not even the muddy roads could prevent these people from kneeling in the most humble and suppliant of attitudes. We reached the holm oak in the Cova da Iria. Once there, moved by an interior impulse, I asked the people to shut their umbrellas and say the Rosary. A little later, we saw the flash of light, and then our Lady appeared on the holm oak."

" 'What do you want of me?'

" 'I want to tell you that a chapel is to be built here in my honor. *I am the Lady of the Rosary. Continue always to pray the Rosary every day.* (Emphasis added.) The war is going to end, and the soldiers will soon return to their homes.'

" 'I have many things to ask you: the cure of some sick persons, the conversion of sinners, and other things....'

" 'Some yes, but not others. They must amend their lives and ask forgiveness for their sins.'

"Looking very sad, our Lady said: 'Do not offend the Lord our God anymore, because he is already so much offended.'

"Then opening her hands, she made them reflect on the sun, and as she ascended, the reflection of her own light continued to be projected on the sun itself.

"This is the reason why I cried out to the people to look at the sun. My aim was not to call their attention to the sun, because I was not even aware of their presence. I was moved to do so under the guidance of an interior impulse.

"After our Lady had disappeared into the immense distance of the firmament, we beheld St. Joseph with the Child Jesus and our Lady robed in white with a blue mantle, beside the sun. St. Joseph and the Child Jesus appeared to bless the world, for they traced the Sign of the Cross with their hands. When, a little later, this apparition disappeared, I saw our Lord and our Lady; it seemed to me that it was Our Lady of Sorrows. Our Lord appeared to bless the world in the same manner as St. Joseph had done. This apparition also vanished, and I saw our Lady once more, this time resembling our Lady of Carmel."

The crowd saw none of this. What the crowd did see was the promised miracle.

The sun stood forth in the clear zenith like a great silver disk. Although it was as bright as any sun they had ever seen, they could look at it without blinking and with a unique and delightful satisfaction. This lasted but a moment. While they gazed, the huge ball began to dance. Now it was whirling rapidly like a gigantic fire wheel. After doing this some time, it stopped. Then it rotated again, with dizzy sickening speed. Finally, there appeared on the rim a border of crimson, which flung itself across the sky...blood-red streamers of flame, reflecting on the earth, on the trees and shrubs, on the upturned faces and the clothes, all sorts of brilliant colors in succession: green, red, orange, blue, violet, the whole spectrum. Madly gyrating in this manner three times, the fiery orb seemed to shudder, and then to plunge in a mighty zigzag toward the crowd.

A fearful cry broke from the lips of thousands of terrified persons as they fell upon their knees, thinking the end of the world had come.

This had lasted about ten minutes. They all saw the sun begin to climb in the same zigzag manner to where it had started. It became tranquil, then dazzling. No one could look at it any longer. It was the ordinary sun of every day.

Not only did some 70,000 people present at the Cova da Iria see this miracle; it was also witnessed many miles away and recorded in the newspapers.

By this miracle our holy Mother seemed to indicate that the apparitions and the messages they contain are for everyone, not just the three shepherd children. There is much from these messages to be learned and put into practice. Our purpose in presenting them here is to point out our holy Mother's emphasis on praying the Rosary. It is clear from these apparitions that the effort for salvation is a cooperative affair. Our prayers, penances and sacrifices are needed in cooperation with heaven, not only for our own salvation but also for that of our fellow sinners. In this effort the Rosary prayer has its important part to play.

Purpose and Use of the Rosary

No Christian prayer form or devotion has had such great popularity and been supported by so many saints, popes, bishops, clergy and laity as the Rosary. It is the only prayer form that has its own feast day, October 7, celebrated by the universal Church.

Throughout its history, the Rosary has had a cyclical life, reaching great heights of popularity and then wavering, only to revive again. During the 20th century, it has seen a rise and decline. This devotion which has evolved from at least the ninth century is so efficacious, so efficient, so capable of helping souls reach great heights of contemplation, so versatile and so pleasing to God, that it merits the most serious attention of all who seek closer union with God.

It is important to focus on the *purpose* of the Rosary, which is simply to help bring us closer to God through and with the Blessed Virgin Mary. Our divine Savior Jesus Christ came to us through Mary. It is God who ordained this, not man. Is it not reasonable, therefore, to take this pathway to God through and with the Blessed Virgin Mary, our holy Mother?

The basis of the Rosary is the "mediatrix" doctrine, so well explained in a document of Vatican II—that the Blessed Virgin Mary is the most powerful intercessor with her Son.

The Rosary is a purely voluntary devotion, but one praised and promoted by the Church. The Church does not *require* its recitation. Just as no one can be forced to believe in and love God, so no one should be required to pray the Rosary. God never forces us, nor does his Church. God has given us free will and he longs for us to come to him, but we must do this of our own volition. The Church he established also shepherds the faithful in this spirit.

It should also be pointed out that the highest form of prayer is the Liturgy of the Mass and the partaking of the "Body, Blood, Soul and Divinity" of our Lord himself in the Holy Eucharist. The Rosary can be said before or after Mass. Its purpose is to bring us to God, and since God is present at Mass, the Rosary has value in preparing our souls to hear his Word and receive him corporally. The Rosary also has a proper place after Mass as a means of thanksgiving. "Eucharist" literally means "thanksgiving," and somewhat like the Samaritan leper who was the only one to return to thank our Lord for curing him, we can use the Rosary to praise and thank God for condescending to come to us with his healing grace.

The Rosary also has a proper place before exposition and Benediction of the Blessed Sacrament, where its role is to help prepare us to receive our Lord spiritually.

The Rosary is so versatile that it can be prayed alone as a private prayer or in groups, either in formal organizations such as the Confraternity of the Most Holy Rosary, or in any *ad hoc* or informal group or gathering. It is particularly suitable as a group prayer of the domestic Church—the family.

Just as the liturgy is a higher form of prayer than the Rosary, so too the Liturgy of the Hours, or what was formerly known as the priest's Breviary, is also considered a higher form of prayer by the Church. The Church encourages the laity to pray the Liturgy of the Hours, and in some places this has taken hold. The Liturgy of the Hours, however, is not as flexible or as readily available as the Rosary. The Rosary can be prayed in a car, or on a bus or airplane, or between household chores. It can be prayed whenever one can snatch the time from his or her daily life. A family, or part of it, can pray the Rosary while driving or walking, or on the beach, or whenever members are alone.

The beauty and genius of the Rosary is that it is always available. It relies on one's memory and on one's desire to meditate. One can be blind and pray the Rosary. One can be imprisoned and pray the Rosary. In communist-controlled countries, which nominally allow Church buildings but punish church-goers, the Rosary can be prayed secretly by a family or by individuals. In this way the reality of religion is maintained. For example, in Lithuania, the Church is allowed to exist, but those who go to church cannot get jobs or go to universities or get apartments. Young people anxious to support themselves and start a family do not attend church. For religion to survive in such a persecution, it must be nourished in the domestic Church, the family. The praying of the Rosary, and the contemplation of the mysteries of the lives of Jesus, Mary and Joseph implant the basic tenets of the Gospel and the faith in the minds of children. As they grow older, they can pray the Rosary silently, even in the midst of a godless society. Similarly, even in free countries one can pray the Rosary in the midst of materialism, the flesh and the world.

Vatican II did not specifically mention the Rosary in its beautiful passages on the Blessed Virgin, but "warmly commended" lawful "popular devotions" of the faithful. Since Vatican II, new prayer methods have been started. These include very worthy prayer groups which emphasize Scripture and the Holy Spirit. Our Lord said, "Whenever two or three gather together...I will be there."

Here is what the American bishops have to say regarding Vatican II and the Blessed Virgin Mary:

"First of all we should clearly understand that the Second Vatican Council in no way downgraded faith in or devotion to Mary. On the contrary, the eighth chapter of the Constitution on the Church is a clear and penetrating account of Catholic teaching on the Blessed Mother of God.... Our Holy Father, Pope Paul VI...called the chapter on our Lady a vast synthesis of Catholic doctrine concerning her place in the mystery of Christ and his Church. He also recalled that she was the heavenly patroness to whom Pope John XXIII entrusted the Council."

The full sense of Mary's role is summed up in the title Pope Paul gave her, "Mother of the Church."

The American bishops implore the faithful to renew

their love for the Blessed Virgin Mary and bare their own hearts to this love and devotion:

"With all the affection of our hearts and the full submission of our minds to the truths of our holy faith, we repeat the Church's familiar words in praise of the Mother of Jesus:

Blessed be the great Mother of God, Mary most holy.
Blessed be her holy and Immaculate Conception.
Blessed be her glorious Assumption.
Blessed be the name of Mary, Virgin and Mother.

"...We proclaim once more the preeminent position of Mary in the mystery of Christ and the Church. We urge the restoration and renewal of the ancient love of Christendom for the Mother of the Lord as a tribute to lay tenderly at her feet.... We pray that she may fill the hearts of all men with peace and lead them to know and love Jesus Christ her Son, and to share in the abundant fruits of his redemption."

The bishops urge the faithful to pray the Rosary:

"It is unwise to reject the Rosary without a trial simply because of the accusation that it comes from the past, that it is repetitious and ill-suited to sophisticated moderns. The scriptural riches of the Rosary are of permanent value. Its prayers, in addition to the opening Apostles' Creed, and the occasional repetition of the ancient and simple doxology (Glory be...), are the Our Father and the Hail Mary. The words of the first half of the Hail Mary are taken from St. Luke. The second half: 'Holy Mary, Mother of God, pray for us sinners, now and at the hour of our death,' is in the mainstream of prayers that go back to the early centuries of Christian devotion."

How to Pray the Rosary

The soul of the Rosary is its meditative prayer. The Angelic Salutation is the background melody for the mind to dwell on the Scriptures. As we have seen in the past, the Rosary was prayed with a thought for each Hail Mary. Whether the thought is announced, such as in group prayer, or reflected on in silence by the individual, this meditative exercise can be used to reach the highest state of contemplation. While concentration on the joyful, sorrowful and glorious mysteries has been the popular emphasis, the Rosary's flexibility permits contemplation of any part of the New Testament.

A Rosary without meditation is like a body without a soul. The beloved Marianist Father George Joseph Meinzinger used to say that there are "Rosarians" and there are "Rattlearians." The latter, of course, are those who merely rattle on without meditating. He also said, "We must pray the Rosary, not say the Rosary,'' and ''A Rosary a day keeps all the devils away,'' and ''Holy Mass and Communion in the morning and the Holy Rosary at night make an awfully good sandwich—you can sandwich everything in between.''

Though aging and ill, this great Rosarian and lover of Mary would drag himself to meetings of the Confraternity of the Most Holy Rosary. He would remark that he would have to be on his deathbed before he missed a Rosary. When, to his chagrin, he had to go to the Marianist home in Cupertino, California, for elderly and ailing priests, he used to dearly miss the opportunity to go to the Confraternity of the Most Holy Rosary or to a Family Rosary meeting. When he led the Rosary he would insist on a perfect cadence, and he would stop the prayer until rhythm was restored. He knew that the Hail Mary was the beautiful music for meditation, and like a good maestro he would seek to urge his players to perfection.

The American bishops have this to say on praying the Rosary and its flexibility:

''The recommended saying of the Rosary does not consist merely in 'telling the beads' by racing through a string of familiar prayers. Interwoven with the prayers are the mysteries. Almost all of these relate saving events in the life of Jesus, episodes in which the Mother of Jesus shared. Nor is rhythmic prayer alien to modern man, as is shown by the attraction of Eastern religions for many young people today. Besides the precise rosary pattern long known to Catholics, we can freely experiment. New sets of mysteries are possible. We have customarily gone from the childhood of Jesus to his passion, bypassing the whole public life. There is rich matter here for rosary meditation, such as the wedding feast of Cana and incidents from the public life where Mary's presence and Mary's name serve as occasions for her Son to give us a lesson in discipleship: 'Still more blessed are they who hear the word of God and keep it' (Luke 11:28)."

The bishops are suggesting that we should not feel compelled to meditate on the Rosary only in a stultified way. The New Testament has much that can be meditated on in addition to the common meditations announced at the beginning of each decade. The Rosary is both a private and a group prayer. In group prayer, there has to be a certain order and rhythm. Otherwise, the sound of the prayer may seem like a cacophony and the form unbalanced to the participants. Even in group Rosary prayer, there can be diversity introduced, such as the announcement of a statement before each decade to stimulate meditation. In individual prayer, time and timing are not as important an element, and more diversity, longer meditation and slower rhythms can be utilized. Each individual is unique, and he or she should be open to the Holy Spirit to guide and lead. He or she should not cut off a thought simply because that is not the way one usually prays the Rosary. One also should not feel compelled to diversify merely for the sake of change. What one should be open to is to increase the depth of his or her prayer—all for the glory of God.

Habit is most important in prayer life. Human beings by nature must lead an ordered life, for they are a creature of a Creator who is the God of order. One should find the place for the Rosary as a part of his or her daily life. For some it is a family prayer best offered at a particular time, such as after dinner. This is a good practice since some, if not all, members of the family are gathered together. For others, it may be praying in a group or individually before or after daily Mass. Some say part of the Rosary while driving a car or whenever else they are alone.

There should not be a spirit of compulsion in praying the Rosary, nor over-emphasis on the number of Rosaries prayed. The Rosary should be a delight to those who pray it. It is a bouquet that we are giving our holy Mother, and she in turn will give it to her Son, who will share it with the Father. A Rosary of five decades well prayed is far superior to fifteen decades which are not. All fifteen decades should be prayed, if possible, but not if they interfere with one's duties in life and are merely said, not prayed, for the sake of getting it done because of the fear of losing some grace. At the same time, it should be recognized that all, even the greatest of saints, experience for varying lengths of time a dryness in prayer. However, this does not mean that we should abandon the Rosary because we no longer receive a desired feeling of joy or consolation.

St. Francis de Sales, a wise director of souls, would not sleep until he had prayed the Rosary. No matter how trying the day or how late it was, he would pray the Rosary. It was his nightcap. It is a good idea to ask St. Joseph and all who love God through and with the Blessed Virgin Mary, to join in praying the Rosary. If we should then fall asleep or for some other reason be unable to finish the Rosary, we need not be overly concerned; St. Joseph and other saints will finish it for us. Remember that God looks into our hearts and it is our intention that is important, not the number of prayers we have completed.

St. Teresa of Avila would become lost in contemplation after praying the words "Our Father...." When she considered the immeasurable love the Father has shown for us by taking us as his children through the redemption and brotherhood of Jesus, she became utterly captivated by this mystery of love. Let us then compare her prayer with that of someone who has said 150 Our Father's but has not given much thought to the words he or she has uttered.

When praying the Rosary, we use the Angelic Salutation for repetitive rhythm. The heart of the Rosary, as we have said, is in its meditation. We need not concentrate and meditate specifically on the Angelic Salutation itself, but rather on the thoughts that well up in our hearts. These give us an insight into Scripture, and more specifically into the life, death and glory of Jesus, Mary his Mother, and Joseph whom he took as his earthly father. When we recite the Glory Be, the Our Father, the "O my Jesus" Fatima prayer, and the Hail Holy Queen, we may concentrate on the meaning of those words.

However, just because we have memorized certain prayers does not mean that we should always utter them without thinking about what they mean. Our prayer life should be constantly renewed, and we should catch ourselves when we find that we are merely uttering sounds. On the other hand, we should not be quick to devalue any form of prayer. If one is disposed to give glory to God and seeks the posture of prayer but his or her powers of concentration are not there for a variety of uncontrollable reasons, that prayer could have immense value. We cannot judge another's prayer—only our own. And sometimes we cannot judge our prayer very well, either. Only God can look into our hearts. We can, however, seek to renew and improve our prayer, and that, of course, is pleasing to God because we seek to better praise and glorify him.

There are times when we can and should meditate on the Angelic Salutation: when it is uttered as a short, spontaneous prayer, for example, or when we are meditating on the Archangel Gabriel's words and those of St. Elizabeth in the joyful mysteries. The second part of the salutation, ''Holy Mary, Mother of God, pray for us sinners,'' has immense value for meditation. The profound meaning of the words ''Mother of God'' (Theotokos) reveals the infinite immensity of God's love for us in his plan of salvation. Consider his choice of this human creature to be the Mother of his Son; that in order to more worthily bear his Son, her soul is created free of original sin; the power she is granted as ''Mother of God''; this power which redounds to our benefit because she can intercede for us with him who is both true God and true Man.

The bishops of the United States have deplored the diminished devotion to our Lady in Catholic prayer life. ''Only a few years ago use of the Rosary was a common mark of a Catholic, and it was customarily taught to children, both at home and in courses of religious instruction. Adults in every walk of life found strength in this familiar prayer which is biblically based and is filled with the thought of Jesus and his Mother in the 'mysteries'.... The praying of the Rosary has declined.... We bishops of the United States wish to affirm with all our strength the lucid statements of the Second Vatican Council on the permanent importance of authentic devotion to the Blessed Virgin Mary, not only in the liturgy, where the Church accords her a most special place under Jesus her Son, but also in the beloved devotions that have been repeatedly approved and encouraged by the Church and that are still filled with meaning for Catholics. As Pope Paul has reminded us, the Rosary and the Scapular are among these tested forms of devotion that bring us closer to Christ through the example and protection of his holy Mother."

Pope Paul VI called the Rosary the "compendium of the entire Gospel," and has referred to his predecessors as having "recommended its frequent recitation, encouraged its diffusion, explained its nature, recognized its suitability for fostering contemplative prayer—prayer of both praise and petition—and recalled its intrinsic effectiveness for promoting Christian life and apostolic commitment....

"We, too, from the first general audience of our pontificate have shown our great esteem for the pious practice of the Rosary.... Since that time we have underlined its value on many different occasions, some ordinary, some grave."

Group Rosary Prayer

My brothers and sisters in Christ, we must recognize what we are up against, we poor fallen children of Eve. *First* we all bear the burden of original sin—something our pure and holy Mother Mary was completely free of. We undergo frequent interior struggles. We are subject to weaknesses. We must fight from falling, not only from outside influences, but merely from our own internal weakness. We are, in reality, poor and weak creatures because of our fallen nature.

Second, we must remember that Lucifer has been allowed to roam the earth. With the victory of our Lord on the cross, Lucifer's sentence has been ratified; he is lost, relegated to hell forever, and he knows it. What he would like to do is to take as many souls with him as he can. That is the nature of evil—to wish evil on another. Good is the opposite—it wishes only the best for another.

And so the evil spirit roams the earth looking for every weakness, attacking from any quarter. Without rest it seeks the ruination of souls.

Third, we have our fellow human beings to contend with. They too are engaged in interior struggles. They too are beset with weaknesses and are a prey for the evil one who is looking for every opportunity to attack. At times they, as we, do not hold the upper hand. They become a danger to us. We cannot find peace with our fellow human beings because they are not at peace with themselves.

Let us thank God for the Immaculate Conception. *Deo gratias* for the Incarnation and the birth of Christ. *Eucharisto Themou* for the life, suffering, death and resurrection of our Lord Jesus. "O Death, where is your victory? O Death, where is your sting?" (1 Corinthians 15:55 RSV) Jesus Christ the Lord has won the victory for us.

But, my dear brothers and sisters in Christ, the last judgment is not yet here. We are a prey to our weakness, the devil, and the frailties of our fellow human beings.

Our Lord and our holy Mother know the condition and situation we are in. That is why Jesus established the Church and why we have the sacraments. That is why the Father and the Son send down the Holy Spirit. That is why we have our holy Mother as our intercessor and protector.

But as we have said before, God has deemed that we must seek him voluntarily. The way we do this is by opening our souls to him through prayer. We implore the Lord for his help and his protection. We ask the Blessed Virgin Mary to intercede for us and to use her God-given powers as Mother and Queen to help and protect us.

Now it stands to reason that praying alone is not as powerful as praying together. An army is stronger than a single soldier. In a group, the entire chorus of prayer, the sum of it, is brought before the throne of God in the hands of our Immaculate Mother.

Not only that, but the value of prayer depends on the state of grace of the person who is praying. The purity of the prayer depends on the condition of the soul who is praying. We have just alluded to our weaknesses and the struggles within the soul. Together we tend to overcome our frailties. The Lord looks into the soul of each individual who is praying and knows the state of grace of every person. The persons in the prayer group who are closest to God enhance the total value of the chorus of prayer offered to God. This is not to suggest that God has a mathematical approach to prayer, but that as he always looks, as a loving God, for the best in us, so too he looks to the best in the group prayer.

The power of praying in a group applies to all prayer. Our concentration here is on the Rosary prayer. We have shown the efficacy of this prayer and how the saints and the popes have recommended it throughout the ages. This powerful prayer to God through his holy Mother becomes even more powerful when prayed in family or in other groups, especially in organizations dedicated to this prayer, such as Rosary Sodalities, Living Rosary Societies, and Confraternities of the Most Holy Rosary. We have alluded to the latter's role in the victory at the battle of Lepanto and in other Christian victories in military battle. The greatest warfare, however, is the battle for souls. This is a spiritual and very real warfare in which the weapon of the Rosary is as powerful and modern today as it was when the Archangel Gabriel uttered the first *Ave.*

It is much easier for the devil to attack one person. Well-organized, devout, group Rosary prayer is like an army of angels which routs the devil and his partners-in-evil.

When an individual, through a voluntary act of his or her will, joins an organization dedicated to devoutly praying, promoting, propagating and defending the Holy Rosary, he or she receives not only immediate benefits but also lasting ones. Such organizations continue to pray for their members both living and dead.

When such a person is suffering, for example, from a terminal illness or serious accident, or is on his death-bed, he receives the same benefits of the Holy Rosary Confraternity as if he were of able body and mind and participating in the group prayer. He derives not only the benefits of the immediate confraternity to which he belongs, but also of all the members who have preceded him to heaven or into the purifying suffering of purgatory.

St. Alphonsus Mary de Liguori says, "It is...preferable to say it [the Rosary] with others rather than alone." He adds, "A confraternity can well be called 'a tower of David; a thousand bucklers hang upon it—all the shields of valiant men' (Canticles 4:4). The reason such societies do so much good is that the members acquire many defensive weapons against hell, and are provided with the means of persevering grace. Those who are not members of confraternities use these weapons and resources only rarely.

"We have already noted how profitable it is for our salvation to serve the Mother of God. But what else do the members of confraternities do except serve her? They praise her. They offer prayers to her. Members are consecrated to her service the moment they join the society. They choose her in a special way as their patroness and protectress. Their names are inscribed in the book of the children of Mary. Every member of a confraternity of Mary can justly say: 'All things together come to me in her company' (Wisdom 7:11). ...Mary looks after all the needs of the members who persevere. 'All her domestics are clothed with double garments' (Proverbs 31:21)."

Pope Leo XIII wrote, "Prayers achieve their greatest efficacy in obtaining God's help when said publicly with perseverance and with one mind by a large number of the faithful, forming as it were one single chorus of suppliants.

"This is clearly indicated in the Acts of the Apostles where it is reported that the disciples of Christ, while awaiting the promised Holy Spirit, 'devoted themselves to constant prayer.'

"Those who pray in this way will never fail to obtain results.

"Such is certainly the case with the members of the Confraternity of the Rosary.

"Just as priests through the recitation of the Divine Office address public, continuous and consequently very efficacious supplications to God, so too the prayers said by the members of this sodality, by reciting the Rosary or the 'Psalter of the Virgin' as several Roman Pontiffs have called it, are in a certain way public, continual and universal.

"Because, as we have said, public prayers are far more preferable than private prayers and enjoy a far greater power of impetration, ecclesiastical writers have called the Confraternity of the Rosary 'the praying army enrolled by St. Dominic under the banner of the Mother of God'—of that Mother of God whom Sacred Scripture and the annals of the Church salute as the conqueror of Satan and of all error.

"In fact, the Rosary unites all those who seek admission into this confraternity as comrades in arms, and in this way constitutes a kind of army properly marshalled and arrayed, able to repel the assaults of our enemies both within and without."

Popes have found that there was no better way to show their high regard for the Confraternity of the Rosary than to join it themselves.

If the Rosary Confraternity is so efficacious as an army against evil, then we must expect that the evil one hates this organization and this prayer and will seek to limit it and its force.

By the 15th century, the Rosary had become neglected. Our holy Mother reportedly appeared to Blessed Alan de la Roche and asked him to revive the Confraternity of the Rosary.

In the 18th century when the Rosary again waned, it was St. Louis Mary de Montfort who became, as the Church called him, "an extraordinary preacher of the Rosary" and a promoter of its confraternity. He wrote: "The Blessed Virgin, Protectress of the Church, has given us a most powerful means for appeasing her Son's anger, uprooting heresy and reforming Christian morals, in the Confraternity of the Holy Rosary...." St. Louis warned Confraternity members against attacks of temptation and of evil. "Dear Confraternity members: if you want to serve Jesus and Mary by saying the Rosary every day, you must be prepared for temptation: 'When you come to the service of God...prepare your soul for temptation' (Ecclesiasticus 2:1). Heretics and licentious folk, 'respectable' people of the world, persons of only surface piety as well as false prophets, hand in glove with your fallen nature and all hell itself, will wage formidable battle against you in an endeavor to get you to give up this holy practice.''

The Rosary and the Confraternity of the Holy Rosary may wane as in the past but will flower again, for their roots are deep in the heart of Mary.

A little story adapted from Queen magazine will emphasize endurance of the Rosary and its confraternity among the North American Indians.

Midway between Montreal and Quebec City, where the St. Maurice River, flowing down from the north, joins the St. Lawrence, a group of French sailors, traders and missionaries landed in 1535.

It was on this Cape, named Cape de la Madeleine, that the Algonquin Indians camped when they brought their furs to St. Maurice, and it was here that the missionaries began teaching the Indians the Rosary.

As early as 1634, the missionaries consecrated this corner of the new world to the Immaculate Conception—some 220 years before this dogma was officially promulgated by Pope Pius IX. Soon after this consecration, the families of the community made it a custom to recite the Rosary in a group. It was here that one of Canada's first Confraternities of the Rosary was started in 1694, and is still active at the shrine today.

When Father Jacques Buteux, who was later martyred by the Iroquois, visited the Akitainegues Indians in 1651, he was delighted to find that each Indian had a rosary and knew his prayers well. He also learned that when a member of the tribe died, his rosary was given to another who would recite the Rosary for the departed. What a wonderful custom and one that we should emulate.

The little parish of Cape de la Madeleine was without a pastor for 150 years. The nation passed from the hands of the Catholic French into the hands of the Protestant English, and the schools, churches and missions that the French had built fell by the wayside.

The faith of the people declined so badly that they forgot their religion. *In spite of this declining faith, the Confraternity of the Rosary endured through the years*—a fact symbolic not only of the power of the Rosary but of the power of group Rosary prayer.

The Family Rosary

Pope Paul VI strongly recommended the recitation of the family Rosary. He saw, as Vatican II pointed out, the Christian family as the "domestic Church" and the Rosary as a common prayer offered to God by the family. Without common prayer the family would lack its character as a domestic Church.

If what the Holy Father said is true, then there must logically follow a concrete effort to reinstate communal prayer in family life if there is to be a revitalization of the theological concept of the family as the domestic Church. Indeed, there is need for greater development of the theology of the family as the domestic Church, as exemplified by the Holy Family itself: the father blessing his wife and children and leading them in prayer; the father and mother offering their children to God, as

Abraham did with Isaac, and the Blessed Virgin Mary did with Jesus; the encouragement of the universal Church to have the Holy Sacrifice of Love in a Home Mass, where Jesus Himself is present in the Holy Eucharist, and the family and the home are blessed by his almighty presence; the practices of blessing the home and consecrating the family to the Sacred Heart of Jesus and the Immaculate Heart of Mary; and to making St. Joseph the head and protector of the house. All these strengthen the family and bind it close to God. The modern practice of calling upon God the Father and God the Son to send the Holy Spirit upon us to cleanse, to renew, to heal, to repair and to energize also belongs, as a pious and holy practice, to the family.

In all of this, the family Rosary should have a powerful and singular role. It is an efficient, holy way of summarizing the Scriptures for children and adults alike and allows for the imaginative and meditative development of faith and piety. It binds the family together in prayer to God, thus strengthening it and bringing upon it God's grace. The family Rosary also therefore protects the family against the world, the flesh and the devil. It is also a means of gaining peace, not as the world gives "peace," but the true peace that God alone can give in the heart. This peace naturally leads to peace among family members. Our holy Mother at Fatima asked the children to pray the Rosary for "peace."

A danger in praying the family Rosary is to say it simply in order "to get it over with." The pressures of time upon family members and the very difficulty of getting the family together all work against the praying of—and indeed the *proper* praying of—the Rosary. Many hours will be spent before the television set, but to take the relatively short time to pray the Rosary seems to some like an excessive burden. Care must be taken that the Rosary will not become drudgery, but rather a prayer of thanksgiving, of petition and of praise.

That great lover of God through the Blessed Virgin Mary, St. Alphonsus Mary de Liguori, wrote: ''The Rosary should be recited as devoutly as possible, and here we may call to mind what the Blessed Virgin said to St. Eulalia: that she was more pleased with five decades said slowly and devoutly than with fifteen said in a hurry and with little devotion. It is well to say the Rosary kneeling before an image of the Blessed Virgin, and before each decade to make an act of love to Jesus and Mary, and to ask them for some special grace. It is also preferable to say it with others rather than alone.''

Who, then, to better pray with than the members of our family? Ideally, all should pray together, but at least one with another, so that we can follow our Lord's advice, ''Again I say to you, if two of you agree on earth about anything they ask, it will be done for them by my Father in heaven. For where two or three are gathered in my name, there am I in the midst of them'' (Matthew 18:19-20 RSV).

Pius XII wrote, ''What form of collective prayer could be more simple and yet more efficacious than the family Rosary, in which parents and children join together in supplicating the eternal Father, through the intercession of their most loving Mother, meditating meanwhile on the sacred mysteries of our faith? There is no surer means of calling down God's blessings upon the family and especially of preserving peace and happiness in the home than the daily recitation of the Rosary. And apart from its supplicatory power, the family Rosary can have very far-reaching effects, for if the habit of this pious practice is inculcated into children at a young and impressionable age, they too will be faithful to the Rosary in later years, and their faith will thereby be nourished and strengthened."

Ways to Pray
the Rosary

There are as many ways to pray the Rosary as there are people who pray it. No one way is really better than another. When praying in a group, there has to be order and similarity. There has to be a sense of rhythm. When praying alone there are a multitude of variations. Even in a group there can be many variations as long as the group prays the audible prayers together.

As we have said, the heart of the Rosary is in the meditative prayer. A Rosary without meditation is like a body without breath. Meditation is familiar conversation with God. When we seek union with God he is pleased to inflame us with his love. Since God is Love, we become immersed in love when we are in union with him.

Meditation does not come easily, because of the demands and distractions of everyday life. A good Christian must have the will to discipline himself—to go to Mass and Communion; to receive the Sacrament of Reconciliation; to refrain from exposing himself to temptation and evil; to perform little acts of mortification; to persevere with fortitude despite trying circumstances.

Meditation, i.e., union with God, takes desire, will and discipline. The Rosary is a disciplined meditation. Without meditation the Rosary can become a clanging of cymbals, a repeating of prayers. But with meditation—as we think about the lives of Jesus, Mary and Joseph; as we meditate on the Sacred Scriptures with our Rosary; as we relate our own lives to God's will for us—we have a magnificent, disciplined meditation, a union with God, a union with Love.

Meditations and their form are limitless. Christians should feel free to use a variety of meditations when praying the Rosary. One should not feel compelled to change his or her method if one feels comfortable with it and has no inclination to change.

If the Rosary is indeed a compendium of the New Testament, then anything contained therein can be meditated on. Further, the lives of Jesus, Mary and Joseph can be related to our own. We can relate to the apostles and to other biblical characters as we see our strengths and weaknesses in them. Our imagination can be developed not only as we see ourselves in biblical scenes but also as we reflect on the meaning of these things as they affect our own lives both now and in the future.

There is much in Scripture that is rich food for meditation as it pertains to Mary and her role in salvation history. She is prefigured in the Old Testament, she blossoms forth in the New Testament, and the Church prunes and develops its insights as in the dogmas of the Immaculate Conception and the glorious Assumption.

The Hail Mary

Mary's Psalter may be recited in several ways, and some may find it advantageous, particularly in private prayer, to utilize several forms.

The first and most prevalent is the traditional: "Hail, Mary, full of grace, the Lord is with you. Blessed are you among women and blessed is the fruit of your womb, Jesus. Holy Mary, Mother of God, pray for us sinners, now and at the hour of our death."

For the first part, a recent translation reads:

"Rejoice, O highly favored daughter! The Lord is with you. Blessed are you among women" (Luke 1:28 NAB, 1970).

Modern scholars consider this a more exact translation. Perhaps some time in the future the Angelic Salutation will be referred to as the "Rejoice" prayer. The emphasis here is that this Servant of the Lord is the highly favored daughter of God the Father. It certainly does not diminish her role or stature in the plan of God as the Mother of his Son.

That Mary is full of grace there is also no doubt, and the traditional salutation does not impugn truth.

We can use the latter in saying the "Hail Mary," which in fact becomes, "Rejoice, O highly favored daughter." Within the Angelic Salutation, Mary, then, is referred to as the "favored daughter" of God as well as the "mother" of God.

The next part of the Hail Mary was first uttered by her kinswoman Elizabeth who was "...filled with the

Holy Spirit and cried out in a loud voice: Blessed are you among women and blessed is the fruit of your womb" (Luke 1:41–42, RSV).

Please note that both the Archangel Gabriel and St. Elizabeth refer to Mary as "blessed" or "blest" among women.

The conclusion of this prayer was given us by the Church when it condemned the Nestorian heresy which taught that Mary was only the Mother of the man Jesus. At the ancient Council of Ephesus in 431 the Church defined the status of the Blessed Virgin Mary as the "Theotokos"—the Mother of God. The Church taught us simply to use this glorious title in prayer by saying:

"Holy Mary, Mother of God, pray for us sinners, now, and at the hour of our death."

If we were to use the modern translation of this prayer to Mary, we would say: "Rejoice, O highly favored daughter. The Lord is with you. Blessed are you among women and blest is the fruit of your womb, Jesus. Holy Mary, Mother of God, pray for us sinners, now and at the hour of our death."

We can go one step further and include Mary's relationship to the third person of the Holy Trinity by reciting the Angelic Salutation as follows: "Rejoice, O highly favored daughter. The Lord is with you. Blessed are you among women and blest is the fruit of your womb, Jesus. Holy Mary, Mother of God, Spouse of God, pray for us sinners, now and at the hour of our death."

Or we can use the traditional salutation for the first part and add reference to her relationship to the Holy Trinity in the last part as follows:

"Hail, Mary, full of grace, the Lord is with you. Blessed are you among women and blessed is the fruit of your womb, Jesus. Holy Mary, *Mother of God, Daughter of God, Spouse of God,* pray for us sinners, now and at the hour of our death."

We are not recommending any particular way. Most will no doubt wish to continue with the Angelic Salutation they are most familiar with. Others may wish to honor Mary, in the Angelic Salutation, not only as the Mother of God but also as his beloved "Daughter" and "Spouse."

St. Louis Mary de Montfort

St. Louis de Montfort suggests a way to help curb distractions and aid in concentration by adding a word or more after the word "Jesus" in the Angelic Salutation, as follows:

Joyful Mysteries

1st Decade—Annunciation: "Jesus incarnate"

2nd Decade—Visitation: "Jesus sanctifying"

3rd Decade—Holy Nativity: "Jesus, born in poverty"

4th Decade—Presentation: "Jesus sacrificed"

5th Decade—Finding in the Temple: "Jesus, Saint among saints"

Sorrowful Mysteries

1st Decade—Agony in the garden: "Jesus in his agony"

2nd Decade—Scourging: "Jesus, scourged"

3rd Decade—Crowning with thorns: "Jesus, crowned with thorns"

4th Decade—Carrying of the Cross: "Jesus, carrying his cross"
5th Decade—Crucifixion: "Jesus crucified"

Glorious Mysteries

1st Decade—Resurrection: "Jesus, risen from the dead"
2nd Decade—Ascension: "Jesus, ascending to heaven"
3rd Decade—Descent of the Holy Spirit: "Jesus, filling you with the Holy Spirit"
4th Decade—Assumption: "Jesus, raising you up"
5th Decade—Coronation: "Jesus, crowning you"

At the end of the Joyful Mysteries, St. Louis suggests we say:

"Grace of the Joyful Mysteries come down into our souls and make them really holy."

St. Louis' longer way which he later modified somewhat, is as follows:

First, say the "Come, Holy Spirit, fill the hearts of your faithful..." and then make your offering of the Rosary:

"I unite myself with all the saints in heaven, and with all the just on earth; I unite myself with you, my Jesus, in order to praise your holy Mother worthily and to praise you in her and by her. I renounce all the distractions that may come to me while I am saying this Rosary.

"O Blessed Virgin Mary, we offer you this Creed in order to honor the faith that you had on earth and to ask you to have us share in the same faith.

"O Lord, we offer you this Our Father so as to adore you in your oneness and to recognize you as the first cause and the last end of all things.

"Most Holy Trinity, we offer you these three Hail Mary's so as to thank you for all the graces which you have given to Mary and those which you have given us through her intercession.

"One Our Father, three Hail Mary's, Glory be...."

How to Offer
Each Decade

The Joyful Mysteries

FIRST DECADE: "We offer you, Lord Jesus, this first decade in honor of your Incarnation, and we ask of you, through this mystery and through the intercession of your most holy Mother, a profound humility."

One Our Father, ten Hail Mary's, Glory be...

"Grace of the mystery of the Incarnation, come down into my soul and make it truly humble."

SECOND DECADE: "We offer you, Lord Jesus, this second decade in honor of the Visitation of your holy Mother to her cousin St. Elizabeth, and we ask of you through this mystery and through Mary's intercession, a perfect charity toward our neighbor."

One Our Father, ten Hail Mary's, Glory be...

"Grace of the mystery of the Visitation, come down into my soul and make it charitable."

THIRD DECADE: "We offer you, Child Jesus, this third decade in honor of your blessed Nativity, and we ask of you, through this mystery and through the intercession of your Blessed Mother, detachment from things of this world, love of poverty and love of the poor."

One Our Father, ten Hail Mary's, Glory be...

"Grace of the mystery of the Nativity, come down into my soul and make me truly poor in spirit."

FOURTH DECADE: "We offer you, Lord Jesus, this fourth decade in honor of your Presentation in the Temple by the hands of Mary, and we ask of you, through this mystery and through the intercession of your Blessed Mother, the gift of wisdom and purity of heart and body."

One Our Father, ten Hail Mary's, Glory be...

"Grace of the mystery of the Purification, come down into my soul and make it wise and pure."

FIFTH DECADE: "We offer you, Lord Jesus, this fifth decade in honor of your Finding in the Temple by our Lady, after she had lost you, and we ask you, through this mystery and through the intercession of your Blessed Mother, to convert us and help us amend our lives, and also to convert all sinners, heretics, schismatics and idolaters."

One Our Father, ten Hail Mary's, Glory be...

"Grace of the mystery of the Finding of the Child Jesus in the Temple, come down into my soul and truly convert me."

The Sorrowful Mysteries

SIXTH DECADE: "We offer you, Lord Jesus, this sixth decade in honor of your mortal Agony in the Garden of Olives, and we ask of you, through this mystery and through the intercession of your Blessed Mother, perfect sorrow for our sins and the virtue of perfect obedience to your holy will."

One Our Father, ten Hail Mary's, Glory be...

"Grace of our Lord's Agony, come down into my soul and make me truly contrite and perfectly obedient to your will."

SEVENTH DECADE: "We offer you, Lord Jesus, this seventh decade in honor of your Bloody Scourging, and we ask of you, through this mystery and through the intercession of the Blessed Mother, the grace to mortify our senses perfectly."

One Our Father, ten Hail Mary's, Glory be...

"Grace of our Lord's Scourging, come down into my soul and make me truly mortified."

EIGHTH DECADE: "We offer you, Lord Jesus, this eighth decade in honor of your cruel crowning with thorns, and we ask of you, through this mystery and through the intercession of your Blessed Mother, the grace to be holy in thought and desire."

One Our Father, ten Hail Mary's, Glory be...

"Grace of the mystery of our Lord's Crowning with Thorns, come down into my soul and make my thoughts holy."

NINTH DECADE: "We offer you, Lord Jesus, this ninth decade in honor of your Carrying the Cross, and we ask of you, through this mystery and through the intercession of the Blessed Mother to give us great patience in carrying our cross in your footsteps every day of our lives."

One Our Father, ten Hail Mary's, Glory be...

"Grace of the mystery of the Carrying of the Cross, come down into my soul and make me truly patient."

TENTH DECADE: "We offer you, Lord Jesus, this tenth decade in honor of your Crucifixion on Mount Calvary, and we ask of you through this mystery and through the intercession of your Blessed Mother, a great horror of sin, a love of the cross and the grace of a holy death for us and for those who are now in their last agony."

One Our Father, ten Hail Mary's, Glory be...

"Grace of the mystery of the Passion and Death of our Lord and Savior, Jesus Christ, come down into my soul and make me truly holy."

The Glorious Mysteries

ELEVENTH DECADE: "We offer you, Lord Jesus, this eleventh decade in honor of your triumphant Resurrection, and we ask of you, through this mystery and through the intercession of your Blessed Mother, a lively faith."

One Our Father, ten Hail Mary's, Glory be...

"Grace of the Resurrection, come down into my soul and make me really faithful."

TWELFTH DECADE: "We offer you, Lord Jesus, this twelfth decade in honor of your glorious Ascension, and we ask of you, through this mystery and through the intercession of your Blessed Mother, a firm hope and a great longing for heaven.''

One Our Father, ten Hail Mary's, Glory be...

"Grace of the mystery of the Ascension of our Lord, come down into my soul and make me ready for heaven.''

THIRTEENTH DECADE: "We offer you, Holy Spirit, this thirteenth decade in honor of the mystery of Pentecost, and we ask of you, through this mystery and through the intercession of Mary, your most faithful Spouse, your holy wisdom, so that we may know, love and practice your truth, and make all others share in it.''

One Our Father, ten Hail Mary's, Glory be...

"Grace of Pentecost, come down into my soul and make me really wise in the eyes of Almighty God.''

FOURTEENTH DECADE: "We offer you, Lord Jesus, this fourteenth decade in honor of the Immaculate Conception and the Assumption of your holy and Blessed Mother, body and soul, into heaven, and we ask of you, through these two mysteries and through her intercession, the gift of true devotion to her, to help us live and die holily.''

One Our Father, ten Hail Mary's, Glory be...

"Grace of the Immaculate Conception and the Assumption of Mary, come down into my soul and make me truly devoted to her.''

FIFTEENTH DECADE: "We offer you, Lord Jesus, this fifteenth and last decade in honor of the glorious Crowning of your Blessed Mother in heaven, and we ask of you, through this mystery and through her intercession, the grace of perseverance and increase of virtue until the very moment of death, and after that the eternal crown that is prepared for us. We ask the same grace for all the just and for all our benefactors."

One Our Father, ten Hail Mary's, Glory be...

"We beseech you, dear Lord Jesus, by the fifteen mysteries of your life, passion and death, by your glory and by the merits of your Blessed Mother, to convert sinners and help the dying, to deliver the holy souls from purgatory and to give us all your grace, so that we may live well and die well. And please give us the light of your glory later on so that we may see you face to face and love you for all eternity. Amen. So be it. GOD ALONE" *(St. Louis Mary de Montfort).*

Another Method

Unite yourself with St. Joseph, the earthly spouse of the Blessed Virgin Mary, and ask him to join you in this prayer and to ask all the saints who love God through, with and for the Blessed Virgin Mary to join you:

In the name of the Father...

I believe in God... (Creed)

Our Father...

Let us pray for an increase and fidelity to faith, hope and love.

Three Hail Mary's or three Rejoice's.

Glory be...

O my Jesus...

O Sacrament most holy...

Joyful Mysteries

1. The Annunciation

Our Father...
The Archangel Gabriel was sent by God to a virgin named Mary in the little town of Nazareth in Galilee.
Hail Mary...

"Rejoice, O highly favored daughter! The Lord is with you. Blessed are you among women."
Hail Mary...

"Do not be afraid, Mary, for you have found favor with God."
Hail Mary...

"For you will bring forth a son and you will call him Jesus and he will be the Son of the Most High."
Hail Mary...

"He will sit on the throne of David his father and rule the House of Jacob forever."
Hail Mary...

"How can this be, since I do not know man?"
Hail Mary...

"The Holy Spirit will come upon you and the power of the Most High will overshadow you and you will conceive."
Hail Mary...

"Know that your kinswoman Elizabeth who has been barren all these years is six months pregnant, for nothing is impossible with God."
Hail Mary...

"Do with me as you say, for I am the servant of the Lord."

Hail Mary...

And the Holy Spirit came upon Mary and she conceived.

Hail Mary...
Come, O Holy Spirit...
Glory be...
O my Jesus...
O Sacrament most holy...

2. The Visitation

Our Father...

Mary resolved to visit her kinswoman Elizabeth, who had been barren all these years and was now pregnant in her old age.

Hail Mary...

And with haste she undertook that long and arduous journey through Galilee, and into the hills of Judea.

Hail Mary...

When Mary greeted Elizabeth she was filled with the Holy Spirit and said, "Blessed are you among women and blest is the fruit of your womb."

Hail Mary...

"And who am I that the mother of my Lord should visit me, for behold at the sound of your voice the babe in my womb leapt with joy."

Hail Mary...

"Blessed is she who believed that the words revealed to her by God would be fulfilled."

Hail Mary...

"My soul proclaims the greatness of the Lord and my spirit rejoices in God my Savior, for he has looked with favor on his lowly servant."

Hail Mary...

"From now on all generations will call me blessed, for he who is mighty has done great things for me and holy is his name."

Hail Mary...

"His mercy is on all those who fear him in every generation, but mighty is his arm as he scatters the proud in their conceit."

Hail Mary...

"The mighty he brings down from their thrones, the lowly he lifts up. The rich he sends away empty, the poor he fills."

Hail Mary...

"And he comes to the help of Israel his servant, for he has remembered his promise of mercy, the promise he made to our fathers, to Abraham and his children forever."

Hail Mary...
Glory be...
O my Jesus...
O Sacrament most holy...

3. The Holy Nativity

Our Father...

Having brought God's blessing to Elizabeth, Zechariah and John the Baptist, Mary stayed about three months and took her leave.

Hail Mary...

On the way home she must have considered the wonderful things God had done for her, and how Saint Joseph, her espoused, would consider her pregnancy. But, having faith, she proceeded.

Hail Mary...

Upon learning of Mary's pregnancy, Joseph resolved to put her away, but quietly because he was a just man.

Hail Mary...

An angel of the Lord came to Joseph in his sleep.

"Joseph, do not be afraid to take Mary as your wife, for the babe in her womb is conceived by the Holy Spirit."

Hail Mary...

"And she will bring forth a son and you will call him Jesus—that is, he who saves."

Hail Mary...

St. Joseph brought Mary into his home, and by bringing Mary into his home he brought Jesus into his home.

Hail Mary...

The time came for the great census and Joseph had to go to Bethlehem to enroll, for he was of the House of David.

Hail Mary...

While in Bethlehem, Mary's time came, and she brought forth her firstborn Son, wrapped him in swaddling clothes and laid him in a manger, because there was no room for them in the inn.

Hail Mary...

An angel of the Lord came to shepherds who were watching their flock at night and said to them, "Behold a savior has been born to you in the city of Bethlehem."

Hail Mary...

"And the wise men came bearing gifts: gold, frankincense and myrrh.

Hail Mary...
Glory be...
O my Jesus...
O Sacrament most holy...

4. *The Presentation*

Our Father...

On the fortieth day Mary and Joseph brought Jesus to the Temple in Jerusalem to present him as the firstborn male.

Hail Mary...

The fortieth day was also that of the purification rites of the Blessed Virgin—she who was pure and immaculate from the first moment of her conception.

Hail Mary...

There was a devout old man named Simeon who was waiting for the consolation of Israel.

Hail Mary...

He took him in his arms and blessed him. "Now you can dismiss me, Lord, for my eyes have seen your salvation, a light to the Gentiles and a glory to your people Israel."

Hail Mary...

"He shall be a sign that will be contradicted and many will rise and fall in Israel because of him."
Hail Mary...

"As for you, a sword will pierce your soul, that the thoughts of many hearts will be revealed."
Hail Mary...

Anna, daughter of Phanuel of the tribe of Asher, who had been widowed seven years after her marriage and spent time in the Temple in prayer and fasting—she too proclaimed him as the Messiah to all who would listen.
Hail Mary...

And the Blessed Virgin Mary pondered these things in her heart.
Hail Mary...

Joseph was warned in a dream by an angel, "Arise, Joseph, and take the child and his mother to Egypt, for Herod seeks to destroy the child."
Hail Mary...

That very night Joseph arose and took them to Egypt: "Out of Egypt I have called my son."
Hail Mary...
Glory be...
O my Jesus...
O Sacrament most holy...

5. Finding of the Child Jesus in the Temple

Our Father...
Jesus, when you were twelve years old, you and your mother and your father, along with other devout Galileans, went up to Jerusalem to celebrate the Passover.
Hail Mary...

When the Passover feast was over, the devout Galileans packed their tents and started home. Unknown to your mother and father you had stayed behind.

Hail Mary...

They had gone one day's journey before they realized you weren't with them, for they thought you were with relatives and friends. They went back to Jerusalem to seek you in great sorrow.

Hail Mary...

When they finally found you after three days, you were in the Temple, listening to the learned doctors of the law and asking them questions. They were amazed at your understanding and your answers.

Hail Mary...

''Son, why have you done so to us? Do you not know that your father and I have been looking for you in great sorrow?''

Hail Mary...

''Why did you seek me? Did you not know I would be in my Father's House?''

Hail Mary...

And you returned with them and were subject to them and grew in age, wisdom and grace before God and man.

Hail Mary...

You blessed family life, work life, business life, social life, church life.

Hail Mary...

You were the high priest of all time, yet you worked as a carpenter; you were a businessman—for you had to sell or barter the things you made; you were a social man—attending weddings and funerals; you were a churchman—attending the synagogue. You were true God and true man.

Hail Mary...

Your holy mother, dear Holy Brother; your holy daughter, dear Holy Father; your holy spouse, dear Holy Spirit—pondered all these things in her heart.

Hail Mary...
Glory be...
O my Jesus...
O Sacrament most holy...

Sorrowful Mysteries

1. *The Agony in the Garden*

Our Father...
You were at the wedding feast in Cana with your disciples when your Mother said to you, "They have no wine."

Hail Mary...

"Woman, what does this concern of yours have to do with me? My hour has not yet come."

Hail Mary...

"Do as he tells you."
Hail Mary...

You took the six jars used for ceremonial washing which held about 15 to 25 gallons each, or 90 to 150 gallons, and had them filled with water. You changed the water into wine.

Hail Mary...

At the request of your Mother, you began your public ministry. You cured us and healed us. You taught us by word and example. You established your Church through your apostles. You gave us your holy Body and Blood, Soul and Divinity through the Holy Eucharist.

Hail Mary...

You took Peter, John and James with you to the Garden at Gethsemane. "Watch here and wait while I pray." Going about a stone's throw away, you lay prostrate and prayed, "Father, if it be your will, let this cup pass from me, but not my will but yours be done."

Hail Mary...

"Could you not watch one hour with me? The spirit is willing but the flesh is weak."

Hail Mary...

"Father, let this cup pass from me, unless it is your holy will. Father, unless it be your holy will, let this cup pass from me."

Hail Mary...

"Judas, you come to betray me with a kiss.... I taught in the Temple and you could have arrested me at any time but now you come to take me like a thief in the night with clubs and swords."

Hail Mary...

"Put your sword away, Peter. Would you not have me drink the cup the Father has given me? He who lives by the sword eventually dies by the sword." They shall strike the shepherd and his sheep will be scattered. They shall strike the shepherd, but not a sheep of his will be harmed.

Hail Mary...

Glory be...

O my Jesus...

O Sacrament most holy...

2. The Scourging

Our Father...

Jesus, they took you to Annas, the father-in-law of Caiaphas, who was high priest that year. Annas, the haughty one with a wide phylactery and flowing tassels.

Hail Mary...

"Tell us about your disciples and your teachings."

"Why do you ask me? Why don't you ask those who heard me, for I taught openly."

Hail Mary...

The guard struck you, my Jesus. He said, "How dare you speak to the high priest that way!"

"If I said evil, bring forth the evidence; otherwise, why do you strike me?"

Hail Mary...

And they brought you to Caiaphas and the Sanhedrin and brought all manner of false witnesses against you, but none would agree.

Hail Mary...

Finally, in desperation they said to you, "We adjure you by the living God, tell us whether you are the Son of the living God."

Hail Mary...

"Your own lips have said it: I am, and from now on you will see the Son of Man sitting at the right hand of the power."

Hail Mary...

And they tore their garments, saying, "He blasphemes; he must die."

Hail Mary...

They brought you to Pilate, who asked, "Are you the king of the Jews?"

You replied, "King is your term. But as you say, I am a king. But my kingdom is not of this world."

"Then you are a king?"

"That is why I was born and why I came into the world, to testify to the truth. Those who are open to the truth hear my voice."

Hail Mary...

"I find no guilt in this man; I will scourge him and let him go." They tied you to the pillar and scourged you.

Hail Mary...

By your stripes we are healed. Lord keep me, keep mine, keep ours, keep us all from the sins of the flesh.

Hail Mary...
Glory be...
O my Jesus...
O Sacrament most holy...

3. The Crowning of Our Lord with Sharp Thorns

Our Father...

Pilate sent you to Herod, who was visiting Jerusalem at the time. He wanted to get rid of you. He knew you were innocent but he was afraid to release you, as he had said, because he was afraid of the Jews.

Hail Mary...

Herod, on the other hand, was anxious to see you because he had heard of your miracles and wanted to see some feat of magic performed.

Hail Mary...

You kept your silence before Herod, that fox, murderer and adulterer, despite many provocations by Herod and his party.

Hail Mary...

Herod sent you back to Pilate dressed in bright robes. Pilate said, "Behold the man." You are true God and true Man, my Lord.

Hail Mary...

"Shall I release to you Barabbas or the king of the Jews?" They preferred Barabbas. Does not the world today still prefer Barabbas?

Hail Mary...

"But I find no guilt in him."

"His guilt be upon us and on our children."

Hail Mary...

Pilate's wife said, "Have nothing to do with that just man, for I have had a dream about him this day."

Pilate asked you, "Who are you? Why don't you answer me? Don't you know I have the power of life and death over you?"

You replied, "You would have no power over me unless it were given you by my Father."

Hail Mary...

"You are no friend of Caesar." As a king they placed you in competition with Caesar. And he gave you over to them. Taking sharp thorns and plaiting them into a crown, they placed it upon your head.

Hail Mary...

And they blindfolded you and hit you, saying, "Prophesy who hit you," and they bent their knees, saying, "Lord, Lord." They spat on you and, taking the reed they had placed in your hand, they hit you with it.

Hail Mary...

You are the King of heaven, yet you are crowned with thorns by man.

Hail Mary...

Glory be...

O my Jesus...

O Sacrament most holy...

4. *Carrying of the Cross*

Our Father...

"If anyone wants to come after me, let him deny himself, pick up his cross and follow me."

Hail Mary...

You fell for the first time, my Lord, under the weight of the cross. You had been scourged and crowned with thorns. You were without food, without drink and without sleep. You had spent the remaining time you had in prayer to God the Father. You were weak and fell but you picked yourself up.

Hail Mary...

You met your afflicted Mother. "Look at me, all you who pass by, and see if there is any sorrow like my sorrow."

Hail Mary...

"I tell you there is no sorrow like my Mother's sorrow. If you took all the sorrow in the world from the beginning of time until the end, it would not equal my Mother's sorrow. Neither would it equal her love."

Hail Mary...

They forced Simon of Cyrene, father of Rufus and Alexander, to help you carry your cross.

Hail Mary...

Veronica wiped your face, my Jesus, and we have devotion to your holy face. Show us your face of love and mercy, O Lord, and we shall be saved.

Hail Mary...

You fell for the second time and picked yourself up. How much, O Lord, did I contribute to your second fall by my own sins, weaknesses and evil inclinations?

Hail Mary...

You met the weeping women of Jerusalem.

"Women of Jerusalem, do not weep for me but weep for yourselves and for your children. For the time will come when you will say, 'Blessed are those who never gave birth and those whose breasts never fed; hills, bury us; and, mountains, fall upon us, for if they do these things in the green wood, what will they do in the dry?"

Hail Mary...

You fell, my Lord, for the third time, and picked yourself up, teaching us that no matter how many times we fall we must pick ourselves up with the help of your patience, perseverance and courage.

Hail Mary...

You offered yourself up as a pure, holy, virginal Lamb of God in reparation for my sins and the sins of all.

Hail Mary...

Glory be...

O my Jesus...

O Sacrament most holy...

5. *Crucifixion*

Our Father...

"Father, forgive them, for they know not what they do."

Hail Mary...

"Woman, behold your son."

Hail Mary...

"Behold, your Mother." Lord, I received the far better part of the bargain. Your Mother received me, a sinner, and I received the holy and immaculate one as my Mother.

Hail Mary...

The good thief said to you, "Lord, remember me when you come into your kingdom." And you said to him, "I tell you, before this day is through I will see you in paradise." My Lord, in your agony you were still forgiving—what love—what mercy!

Hail Mary...

"My God, my God, why have you forsaken me?"
Hail Mary...

"I thirst."
Hail Mary...

"It is finished."
Hail Mary...

"Father, into your hands I commend my spirit." Lord, into your hands I commend my spirit.
Hail Mary...

The sun darkened, the earth quaked and the Temple curtain was torn in two. "Truly, this is the Son of God."
Hail Mary...

The Roman soldier thrust a lance into your side, and blood and water came out—you gave the last drop of blood and water you had out of love for us. And a sword pierced our holy Mother's soul, that the thoughts of many hearts may be revealed. She gave herself totally.

Hail Mary...
Glory be...

O my Jesus...
O Sacrament most holy...

Glorious Mysteries

1. The Resurrection

Our Father...

The holy women were on their way to the tomb to anoint your body, dear Jesus. There had not been enough time for proper preparation of your body with spices and ointments because the sun had gone down on the eve of the Passover feast.

Hail Mary...

They wondered how they were going to remove the large stone in front of the tomb, but having faith they proceeded.

Hail Mary...

When they reached the tomb, the stone had been removed. Their faith had been justified.

Hail Mary...

An angel of the Lord appeared to them and said, ''You are looking for Jesus of Nazareth. He has risen as he foretold. He goes before you into Galilee. Go and tell Peter and the others.''

Hail Mary...

They did this, and Peter and John rushed to the tomb in that famous foot race. John outran Peter and got to the tomb first.

Hail Mary...

John peered into the tomb but did not enter. When Peter reached the tomb, he went in and saw the wrappings of the body and the cloth which covered our Lord's face—all neatly folded.

Hail Mary...

Then John entered, and seeing, he believed. Up until then they had not understood the resurrection.

Hail Mary...

Mary Magdalene stood at the tomb, weeping. An angel of the Lord asked her, "Woman, why are you weeping?"

"They have taken my Lord away and I don't know where they have taken him."

Then you, O Lord, said to her, "Woman, why are you weeping?"

"They have taken my Lord away. If you have taken him, tell me where he is and I will go and get him."

Hail Mary...

"Mary."

"Rabbi."

"Do not cling to me for I have not yet ascended to my Father."

Hail Mary...

"Go and tell my brethren. I go to my Father and their Father, to my God and to their God."

Hail Mary...

Glory be...

O my Jesus...

O Sacrament most holy...

2. The Ascension

Our Father...

You appeared, O Lord, to Cleopas and his companion on their way to Emmaus. You asked them, "What is this discussion you are having as you walk along the way?"

Hail Mary...

"Are you the only one in Jerusalem who has not heard of Jesus of Nazareth, a great prophet who was crucified? We thought he was going to restore the kingdom."

"Oh, how slow you are to believe; did you not know the Christ would have to suffer before he went to his glory?"

Hail Mary...

And you explained to them all the scriptures pertaining to yourself. And they said, "The hour is late; come and stay with us." At the evening meal you blessed the bread, broke it and gave it to them. They recognized you at the breaking of the bread. "Were not our hearts on fire when he was with us?"

Hail Mary...

You appeared to your apostles. "Peace be with you. Do not be afraid. It is I, the Lord. Have you anything to eat?"

Hail Mary...

"Here, put your finger into my hands and your hand into my side. See and believe. Blessed are those who do not see, yet believe."

Hail Mary...

"Cast your nets on the starboard side." They did and caught 153 fish. There are 153 Hail Mary's in the fifteen decades of the rosary.

Hail Mary...

"Simon Peter, do you love me more than these do?"
"Yes, Lord."
"Feed my lambs."
Hail Mary...

"Simon Peter, do you love me?"
"Yes, Lord."
"Tend my sheep."
Hail Mary...

"Simon Peter, do you love me?"
"Yes, Lord, you know that I love you. You know all things."
"Feed my sheep."
Hail Mary...

"Now I must go. You do not ask where I am going. I go to prepare a place for you. If I do not go, I will not be able to send you the Holy Paraclete. Go into the city and wait."

Hail Mary...
Glory be...
O my Jesus...
O Sacrament most holy...

3. *The Descent of the Holy Spirit*

Our Father...

They were in the upper room with the Blessed Virgin Mary, the spouse of the Holy Spirit, with the doors barred in fear of the Jews.

Hail Mary...

They were praying for the Holy Spirit. "Come, O Holy Spirit, come. Come, O Holy Spirit, come."

Hail Mary...

Suddenly there was a sound as of a violent wind blowing, and there appeared tongues as of fire which parted and settled on each of them.

Hail Mary...

Filled with the Holy Spirit, they threw open the doors, went into the city and praised God and his Son, Jesus of Nazareth.

Hail Mary...

And they were able to speak in every tongue and all were amazed that they could understand them no matter what language they spoke.

Hail Mary...

Some said, "Are these not Galileans? They must be drunk!"

Hail Mary...

But Simon Peter went up the steps of the Temple and said, "Men of Jerusalem, listen to me. These men are not drunk as you suppose. It is only 9 o'clock in the morning. They are filled with the Holy Spirit."

Hail Mary...

He explained all the scriptures pertaining to you, my Jesus, saying finally, "And when he came, what did you do? You hung him on a cross."
Hail Mary...

"They were cut to the heart and said, "What shall we do, brothers?" Peter replied, "Repent and be baptized."
Hail Mary...

On that day, some three thousand were baptized.
Come, O Holy Spirit, fill the hearts of your faithful and kindle in them the fire of your love. Send forth your spirit and they shall be created, and you shall renew the face of the earth.
Hail Mary...
Glory be...
O my Jesus...
O Sacrament most holy...

4. The Assumption

Our Father...
You are sweeter than honey, better to have than the honeycomb.
Hail Mary...

You are like a rainbow in the cloudy sky.
Hail Mary...

You are like an early blossom in springtime.
Hail Mary...

You are the glory of Jerusalem.
Hail Mary...

You are the joy of Israel.
Hail Mary...

You are the honor of our people.
Hail Mary...

Look, O daughter, and see; turn your ear; leave your family, for the king shall desire your beauty. You shall worship the Lord your God.
Hail Mary...

And God raised you up to heaven with his love.
Hail Mary...

And behold a sign appeared in heaven, a woman clothed with the sun, and the moon was under her feet, and upon her head, a crown of twelve stars.
Hail Mary...

And you took your place at the right hand of your Son.
Hail Mary...
Glory be...
O my Jesus...
O Sacrament most holy....

5. *The Coronation*

Our Father...
You are the Queen of heaven, of earth, and of all God's creation, because you are the beloved Daughter of God the Father, the beloved Mother of God the Son, and the beloved Spouse of the Holy Spirit.
Hail Mary...

You are the Queen and Advocate of sinners. Please be my advocate.

Hail Mary...

You are the Queen of the poor, the Queen of the suffering, the Queen of all that is good.

Hail Mary...

You are our life, our sweetness and our hope. You are the Mother of fair love, of fear, of knowledge and of holy hope.

Hail Mary...

You are Our Lady of Peace, the Queen of Peace. Please grant us the peace of God.

Hail Mary...

You are Our Lady of Grace, the fountain of all grace, the mediatrix of all grace. You whom God calls full of grace, please fill us with the holy grace of God.

Hail Mary...

Queen of the most holy Rosary, our Lady of the most holy Rosary, please teach us how to pray the Rosary well. May it be a bulwark against evil, both visible and invisible, and a way through your most Immaculate Heart to the most Sacred Heart of Jesus.

Hail Mary...

Through the scapular that we wear, we rededicate ourselves as slaves to the most Sacred Heart of Jesus through slavery to your most Immaculate Heart.

Hail Mary...

Hail, O Queen of mercy, protect us from the enemy and receive us at the hour of our death. My Mother and my Queen!

Hail Mary...

Mother and Queen of the Church militant, the Church suffering, and the Church triumphant, have mercy on me, a poor sinner.

Hail Mary...
Glory be...
O my Jesus...
O Sacrament most holy...
Hail holy Queen...

The Dynamic Rosary

In the chapter on the "History of the Rosary" we traced the development of the Rosary to its present form. The Rosary should not and will not cease to develop further, meeting the needs of the particular times. Today, Catholics are much more knowledgeable about Scripture than they have been in the past. The richness and the beauty of the Old and New Testaments can be melded into Rosary prayers and meditations As we develop new knowledge and insights on the scriptures, our Rosary meditations can be adapted to work these into our Rosary prayer. A Christian is a dynamic individual filled with the Holy Spirit. He grows in his Christianity—he is not static or stunted, but grows ever closer to God.

The Rosary prayer grows along with the growth of the Christian. This is not to say that the Rosary prayer of today or tomorrow is better than the Rosary prayer of yesterday. It is that one's Rosary prayer of today meets the needs of today, just as the Rosary prayers of yesterday met the needs of those times. God does not evaluate our prayer in terms of the correctness of certain words or on whether we are meditating on an updated translation of the Bible. He looks into our hearts and our intentions. In any case, the great value of the Rosary is that since it is Mary's special prayer it is taken by her and given to God. A prayer from Mary's lips increases its value not seven times but seventy times seven. In other words, we cannot measure its value.

Bibliography

Alphonsus Mary de Liguori, St. *The Glories of Mary*. Baltimore, MD: Helicon Press, Inc., 1963. Part Two, Sermons and Meditations.

Bourke, Simon, SM. *Homily*. Confraternity of Our Lady of Mount Carmel, Star of the Sea Church, Honolulu, November 5, 1983.

Butler's Lives of the Saints, Vol. IV, ed., revised and supplemented by Herbert Thurston, SJ, and Donald Attwater. Westminster, MD: Christian Classics, Inc., 1956.

Carthusian. *A Month With Mary*. Springfield, IL: Temple Gate.

Clement XIII. Apostolic Letter *Ad Augendam*. November 18, 1795.

The Documents of Vatican II, ed. Walter M. Abbott, SJ. Oak Park, IL: American Catholic Press, Inc., 1963.

Gregory XVI. Apostolic Letter *Benedicentes*. January 27, 1832.

Holy Rosary—Papal Teachings, selected and arranged by the Benedictine Monks of Solesmes. Boston: St. Paul Editions, 1980.

John XXIII. Apostolic Letter II *Religioso Convegno*. September 29, 1961.

_____. Allocution to the First Pilgrimage of the Living Rosary. May 4, 1963.

John Paul II. Angelus Message of October 29, 1978.

_____. *England, Scotland, Wales: Unity—God's Gift*. Boston: St. Paul Editions, 1983.

_____. *Portugal: Message of Fatima*. Boston: St. Paul Editions, 1983.

Korn, Frank J. *Country of the Spirit: Vatican City*. Boston: St. Paul Editions, 1982.

LeBlanc, Sr. Mary Francis, O.Carm. *Cause of Our Joy*. Boston: St. Paul Editions, 1976.

Leo XIII. Encyclical *Supremi Apostolatus*. September 1, 1883.

Louis Mary de Montfort, St. *True Devotion to the Blessed Virgin Mary*. New York: Alba House, 1973.

_____. *The Secret of the Rosary*. Bayshore, NY: Montfort Publications, 1973.

Lucia, Sr., *Fatima in Lucia's Own Words (Memoirs)*, ed. Fr. Louis Kondor, SVD, and trans. Dominican Nuns of the Perpetual Rosary. Fatima, Portugal: Postulation Centre, May 1976.

National Council of Catholic Bishops. *Behold Your Mother, Woman of Faith*. A Pastoral Letter on the Blessed Virgin Mary, 1973.

Norton, Richard F. *Visitations of Our Lady*. 1946.

Paul VI. Apostolic Exhortation *Marialis Cultus*. Vatican translation. Society of St. Paul, 1974; also United States Catholic Conference, 1974.

_____. Allocution to the Children of the Living Rosary. May 10, 1964.

_____. Allocution to the General Audience. October 7, 1964.

_____. Encyclical *Christi Matri*. September 15, 1966.

Pius V, St. Brief *Consueverunt Romani, Pontifices*. September 15, 1569.

_____. *Salvatoris Domini*. March 5, 1571.

Pius IX. Apostolic Letter *Postquam, Deo Momente*. April 12, 1867.

_____. Apostolic Letter *Eregus Sues. December 3*, 1869.

_____. Apostolic Letter *C'est un Fait Eclant*. To the Superior and Missionaries of the Sanctuary of Lourdes. February 8, 1875.

Pius X, St. Letter *Novinus ex it Ureuu*. To Rev. Ignatius Body, OP. June 27, 1908.

Pius XII. Letter to Bernard Cardinal Griffin, Archbishop of Westminster. July 14, 1952.

Queen magazine. May–June, 1979.

Scriptural Rosary. Chicago, IL: Scriptural Rosary Center, 1963.

Seventeen Papal Documents on the Rosary. Boston: St. Paul Editions.

Thorton, Francis Beauchesne. This is the Rosary. New York: Hawthorn Books, Inc., 1961.

Walsh, William Thomas. Our Lady of Fatima. New York: The Macmillan Co., 1947.

About the Author

Andrew J. Gerakas was born in 1928, in New York City, of Greek Orthodox immigrant parents. It was from them that he first learned to love the Blessed Virgin Mary, or *Panayia* as the Greeks call her. Although ordained in the Roman Catholic Church, he does not feel that he has left one Church for the sake of the other. He believes that the very deep devotion and love that both Churches have for the Mother of God and the Mother of all will be a unifying influence that will eventually bring Orthodox and Catholic together. He has written a treatise on the "Holy Eucharist in the Orthodox and Roman Catholic Churches," exhorting unity at the Lord's Table.

Deacon Gerakas is currently assigned to the Cathedral of Our Lady of Peace in Honolulu. He started and heads a number of organizations in Honolulu with special devotion to God through the Blessed Virgin Mary, including The Confraternity of the Most Holy Rosary and The Confraternity of Our Lady of Mount Carmel.

St. Paul Book & Media Centers

ALASKA
750 West 5th Ave., Anchorage, AK 99501 907-272-8183.
CALIFORNIA
3908 Sepulveda Blvd., Culver City, CA 90230 310-397-8676.
1570 Fifth Ave. (at Cedar Street), San Diego, CA 92101 619-232-1442
46 Geary Street, San Francisco, CA 94108 415-781-5180.
FLORIDA
145 S.W. 107th Ave., Miami, FL 33174 305-559-6715; 305-559-6716.
HAWAII
1143 Bishop Street, Honolulu, HI 96813 808-521-2731.
ILLINOIS
172 North Michigan Ave., Chicago, IL 60601 312-346-4228; 312-346-3240.
LOUISIANA
4403 Veterans Memorial Blvd., Metairie, LA 70006 504-887-7631; 504-887-0113.
MASSACHUSETTS
50 St. Paul's Ave., Jamaica Plain, Boston, MA 02130 617-522-8911.
Rte. 1, 885 Providence Hwy., Dedham, MA 02026 617-326-5385.
MISSOURI
9804 Watson Rd., St. Louis, MO 63126 314-965-3512; 314-965-3571.
NEW JERSEY
561 U.S. Route 1, Wick Plaza, Edison, NJ 08817 908-572-1200.
NEW YORK
150 East 52nd Street, New York, NY 10022 212-754-1110.
78 Fort Place, Staten Island, NY 10301 718-447-5071; 718-447-5086.
OHIO
2105 Ontario Street (at Prospect Ave.), Cleveland, OH 44115 216-621-9427.
PENNSYLVANIA
214 W. DeKalb Pike, King of Prussia, PA 19406 215-337-1882; 215-337-2077.
SOUTH CAROLINA
243 King Street, Charleston, SC 29401 803-577-0175.
TEXAS
114 Main Plaza, San Antonio, TX 78205 512-224-8101.
VIRGINIA
1025 King Street, Alexandria, VA 22314 703-549-3806.
CANADA
3022 Dufferin Street, Toronto, Ontario, Canada M6B 3T5 416-781-9131.